GARDENING WITH

ferns

GARDENING WITH

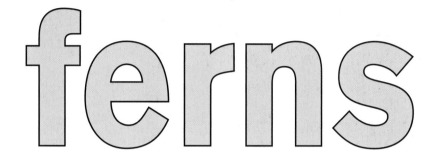
ferns

MARTIN RICKARD

A HORTICULTURE BOOK

Horticulture Publications, Boston, Massachusetts

First published in the US in 2005 ISBN 1-55870-762-X

Horticulture is a subsidiary of F+W Publications Inc. Company
Distributed by F+W Publications Inc.
4700 East Galbraith Road, Cincinnati, OH 45236
1-800-289-0963

Printed in Singapore by KHL Printing Co Pte Ltd
for Horticulture Publications, Boston, Massachusetts

Visit our website at www.hortmag.com

Some of the material in this book has previously appeared in *The
Plantfinder's Guide to Ferns* by Martin Rickard.

PRACTICAL PROJECTS
Designed and described by Jo Weeks

PICTURE ACKNOWLEDGMENTS
Photos by Marie O'Hara and Martin Rickard
Illustrations by Coral Mula
Planting plans by Ethan Danielson

NOTE: Throughout the book the time of year is given as a season to make the reference applicable to readers all over the world. In the
northern hemisphere the seasons may be translated into months as follows:

Early winter **December**	*Early spring* **March**	*Early summer* **June**	*Early autumn* **September**
Midwinter **January**	*Mid-spring* **April**	*Midsummer* **July**	*Mid-autumn* **October**
Later winter **February**	*Late spring* **May**	*Late summer* **August**	*Later autumn* **November**

CONTENTS

Why Ferns?

Whether in a mixed border, beside water, in containers or in a dedicated fernery, ferns have a place in gardens. They are second to none when it comes to adorning difficult shady corners, and virtually all gardens have such places, frequently embellished with only a dustbin. But there are also ferns that will grow in sunnier sites among perennials and shrubs and those that enjoy a damp situation beside a pond or stream.

The short description of a fern is a plant with bracken-like, much divided fronds, but the range within this basic form is staggering. There are crested types with attractive tassles at their tips, more feathery varieties in which the lacy texture is amplified, and fronds in which the blade is entire (not cut at all). These latter, uncut fronds are usually leathery and thick-textured, contrasting beautifully with the delicate filigree fronds of the archetypal forms. Frond shape is not the only variable: the addition of a trunk, as with the tree ferns, adds a completely different dimension.

Dryopteris neorosthornii

What is a fern?

True ferns are the principal components of the plant group known as the Pteridophyta. In an evolutionary sense the Pteridophyta fit between the Bryophyta (mosses and liverworts) and the Gymnospermae (conifers or gymnosperms). Of all the plants known today, the Pteridophyta are the most primitive with vascular tissue (tubular cells that carry food and moisture around the plant). The more primitive mosses and liverworts lack vascular tissue and are, therefore, very limited in size. Ferns reproduce by spores, which are usually brown or green and formed on the underside of the fronds (see Propagation, pp. 18–21).

The appeal of ferns

The majority of ferns are green, but what a range of green! Forty shades is not an exaggeration. In addition to shades of green there is reflectiveness: while many fronds are matt, some are glossy, particularly those of *Asplenium scolopendrium*. Some ferns have hairs on the fronds, which enhance their appearance, especially when the fronds are unfurling: *Polystichum polyblepharum* is an example. Similarly scales on the rachis and stipe, such as those on *Cyathea australis*, can also be beautiful. Coloured scales are even better. The black-scaled new fronds of *Dryopteris neorosthornii* or the brown scales of some forms of *D. wallichiana* have quite an impact.

Many Asian species have coloured fronds. *Athyrium niponicum* 'Pictum' is a favourite with grey fronds that have a mauve central section. *Athyrium otophorum* can be even more striking. Its fronds are yellow-green with a bright red rachis and main veins, while another lady fern, *A. vidalii*, has a dark red rachis and veins and a green lamina. Another Asian species, *Adiantum aleuticum* 'Japonicum', has staggeringly beautiful red fronds in spring.

Osmunda regalis 'Purpurascens' has red fronds in spring while the rachis and other midribs stay red throughout the season. *O. regalis* var. *spectabilis* can also be reddish in spring but eventually turns green. In the native populations in western Europe, red-tinged forms of *O. regalis* can be found, especially towards the south and west.

Dryopteris erythrosora is a tough plant with bright red new fronds in spring. These turn bronze within a week or two, becoming green a month or so later, but the plant continues to produce new red fronds through most of the season. In addition to this flushing of red, *D. erythrosora* rings the changes through winter. It is evergreen in all but the severest winters and the overwintering fronds turn an attractive yellow. While *D. erythrosora* has triangular, bipinnate fronds, *D. lepidopoda* has lanceolate pinnate-pinnatifid fronds that are also red in spring. Another species flushing red then bronze is *Woodwardia unigemmata*. It can have fronds of 2m (6ft) – a spectacular sight in spring. *Blechnum* also has species that flush red in spring.

There are rare much desired forms of *Asplenium scolopendrium* Crispum Group that are naturally striped at random with broad yellowish green bands between the normal green areas. 'Golden Queen' and 'Variegatum Bolton' are two such cultivars. This effect is best brought out in dappled sun, preferably not full sun around midday as some leaf scorch may occur. In deep shade the variegation may not develop. *Dryopteris dickinsii* is one of a selection of ferns that are often a pale green approaching yellowish green.

Although ferns do not have flowers, the diversity in their frond shapes and sizes, shades of green and distinct textures is surely more than adequate compensation for all but the least discerning of gardeners.

Caring for Ferns

As with many other plants, growing ferns is easy so long as their basic cultivation requirements – site, moisture, food and sunlight or shade – are taken into account. There are many different ferns with a wide range of cultural requirements and varieties can be found to suit most sites and conditions.

What site?

Far right: Asplenium trichomanes is happy growing in the cracks in dry stone walls.

Below: Matteuccia struthiopteris in a mixed border with Tropaeolum speciosum and hostas, making a lush display under trees.

In damper parts of the temperate world where ferns abound, they are usually found in well-drained sites. For example, in south-west England, ferns such as *Polystichum setiferum, Asplenium scolopendrium, Asplenium trichomanes* and various species of *Dryopteris* are luxuriant on roadside banks and are often the dominant plant in such habitats. These banks consist of stones and debris that have been cleared off the surrounding land over many years. The result is a site with good drainage and a fertile growing medium, conditions ferns love.

The average garden border – moist but well-drained – fits the bill for most ferns, and it is even better if it is sheltered and shady. Even more perfect is a slight slope where conditions mimic those of a roadside bank as described above. Establishment may require a little extra care in this case but, once they are growing well, the

ferns can be wonderfully successful. One problem that may occur before the plants are fully established is erosion of the soil by rain or heavy watering. Erosion will remove the topsoil and expose some of the plant's roots, with the result that the plant becomes insecure in its position. It is, therefore, a good idea to plant into a depression in the bank. As rain falls, soil from above will gradually wash down onto the fern rootstock and will eventually fill the depression and firm in the plant.

Ferns also grow well in a woodland garden. Here, the canopy is important. If it is very dense, the ferns will not receive enough moisture. Large overhead trees such as oak and birch are perfect as long as they are well spaced with roots at a reasonable depth. Hawthorn and many smaller ornamental trees are also good; however, suckering species like flowering cherries are less suitable as the surface roots compete with the ferns for water. Rhododendrons and other large shrubs are fine, especially if it is possible to plant the ferns between them rather than under them. Heavy-shade casters such as beech and yew can be a challenge: to thrive,

ferns need to be positioned at the edge of their umbrage. *Polypodium australe* and its wonderful cultivars can do well under deciduous trees as all prefer dryish conditions without too much humidity; they also die down during late spring and early summer, so are not about when the shade is at its heaviest, and grow new fronds in the autumn when the tree leaves drop. Soil type plays a part. Ferns under trees on lighter sandy or peaty soil may struggle more than those on heavy clay, which is excellent at retaining water.

Asplenium scolopendrium has wonderful glossy leathery leaves and is at its best on and beside banks and walls.

Polypodium australe 'Cambricum Willharris' survives well under trees as it becomes dormant before they are in full leaf and so is unaffected by the dry conditions that prevail then.

Ferns for rockeries

All the ferns for dry conditions can be grown in rockeries. The following are also good:

Asplenium trichomanes and cultivars
Cystopteris fragilis and other cystopteris
Davallia mariesii
Woodsia obtusa
Woodsia polystichoides

Ferns for dryish shade

Dryish means slightly moist, not dust, preferably woodland.

Adiantum aleuticum
Adiantum x mairisii
Adiantum pedatum
Adiantum venustum, and all other hardy adiantums
Arachniodes standishii
Asplenium scolopendrium and cultivars
Cyrtomium fortunei and other cyrtomiums
Dryopteris most
Paesia scaberula
Polypodium australe
Polypodium interjectum
Polypodium vulgare and all other polypodiums
Polystichum species
Polystichum setiferum cultivars

Ferns for very wet conditions

Athyrium species
Athyrium filix-femina cultivars
Dryopteris cristata
Matteuccia struthiopteris
Onoclea sensibilis
Osmunda species
Osmunda regalis cultivars
Thelypteris palustris
Todea barbara
Woodwardia areolata
Woodwardia virginica

Ferns for moderately wet sites

Blechnum spicant and other blechnums
Gymnocarpium dryopteris
Phegopteris connectilis

Sun or shade?

Ferns generally prefer shade, particularly during the hottest times of the day: noon to 3.00pm. Although some can put up with such exposure, they will be somewhat less luxuriant. Many species of dryopteris, especially *Dryopteris affinis* and its cultivars, can, however, do well in sunny spots. In fact nearly all ferns that like reasonably good drainage will endure full sun (*Asplenium scolopendrium* cultivars are an exception, see below). Even wet-loving ferns can be happy in sun if they are provided with adequate water: *Osmunda regalis* thrives in full sun at the RHS garden at Wisley where it is planted on the edges of lakes and water courses. The soft tree fern *Dicksonia antarctica* does well in a sunny site but has shorter leaves as a result.

Full sun can be damaging to the thin-textured fronds of cultivars of the *Asplenium scolopendrium* Crispum Group. These become unnaturally yellow, and brown blotchy burn marks can appear on them. 'Golden Queen', a rather rare form in the Crispum Group, is naturally streaked yellow – the character is enhanced if it is planted in a bright spot but it is still best out of direct sun during the midday period. Fronds of any fern that has been grown

Dryopteris affinis can survive in a reasonably sunny spot.

in a cool shady site are almost certain to burn badly if they are suddenly exposed to sun; subsequent fronds will be healthy if sufficient water is provided.

Wind?

Like full sun, wind exposure is best avoided. Delicate fern fronds can be snapped and distorted by wind, defeating the object of growing them in the first place. Young fronds that are blown about can snag on each other, turning black at the tips and reducing the beauty of the frond when fully unfurled. One of the worst ferns for a windy site is *Adiantum aleuticum*: its fronds are fan-shaped and top heavy, readily catching the wind and snapping very

The delicate fronds of *Asplenium scolopendrium* Fimbriatum Group are easily damaged by sun.

Desert ferns

Some ferns are hardy but cannot tolerate winter wet, which is prevalent in cool-temperate zones, such as the British Isles. Notable examples are species of cheilanthes and pellaea, most which are best grown in an alpine house. However, *Cheilanthes tomentosa* (right) will grow outdoors in central England if provided with very good drainage and some overhead winter protection for the crown to keep off the worst of the rain. Desert ferns are among the few that would be worth trying on a south-facing sunny bank (the least suitable site for ferns) if these preferred growing conditions can be met.

easily. However, small leathery-fronded species, such as asplenium, and leathery epiphytic microsoriums are rarely affected by wind.

Ferns that prefer acid soil

Those marked * particularly prefer acid conditions (see also A–Z of Ferns pp.25–85).

Asplenium septentrionale and several other aspleniums*
Blechnum (all species)*
Cheilanthes (some)
Gymnocarpium dryopteris
Osmunda regalis
Paesia scaberula
Pellaea (some)
Phegopteris connectilis
Polypodium vulgare
Woodsia (some)
Woodwardia virginica

Note: Although *Osmunda regalis* may prefer acid soil, it is far from crucial. Sizergh Castle in Cumbria has the National Collection of Osmunda and it is planted out in a large rockery created from water-washed limestone. Natural streams run through the garden and the water is presumably alkaline.

Ferns that prefer alkaline soil

Those marked * particularly prefer alkaline conditions (see also A–Z of Ferns, pp.25–85).

Asplenium scolopendrium and cultivars, and many other asplenium species*
Cystopteris fragilis and most other species*
Gymnocarpium robertianum
Polystichum aculeatum
Polystichum setiferum and cultivars
Polypodium australe

Note: *Asplenium scolopendrium* tends not to do well in very acid gardens.

Ferns indifferent to soil pH

Adiantum (most)
Cyrtomium
Dryopteris (most)

Soil

Most of the popular garden ferns are either calcicole (lime lovers) or totally indifferent to all but very extreme soil pH. (pH is a measurement of acidity: pH 7 is neutral, with higher numbers progressively more alkaline and lower numbers progressively more acidic.) The few true calcifuges (lime-haters) can be grown satisfactorily in limy gardens by importing an ericaceous compost. For those gardening on pure chalk, it is probably best to prepare a special bed for calcicoles, excluding the chalk substrate by lining it with polythene.

Soil drainage is usually more important than pH and can influence the choice of species to grow. Sandy soils are free draining and usually need to have their moisture-retaining properties improved by adding fibre in the form of peat, coir, leaf mould or well-rotted garden compost. The same organic materials can be added to very heavy soils, as they open up the soil structure and prevent waterlogging. Ferns enjoy heavy clay: there is always some moisture available in it, even in serious drought when cracks appear on the surface. The blocks of apparently dry soil are protecting the remaining moisture, and established ferns are able to reach it. I have no experience of growing ferns on peaty soil, but I am sure it would suit them well. Again the addition of well-rotted compost will improve its structure.

Feeding

In the garden, fertilizer is not really necessary for ferns, but can be added to achieve greater luxuriance. Well-rotted animal manure is an excellent conditioner and provides nutrients – 3–4-year-old horse manure is good. Seaweed fertilizers are also recommended. Beware of giving too much fertilizer as this can encourage excessive foliar growth at the expense of the roots, which means the fronds will be weak and the plants quickly affected by drought.

Pot-grown ferns require feeding. Slow-release granules used each spring will feed a pot for a whole year and it is a good idea to add some granules to the mix when potting on in spring; if you are potting on in autumn, omit the granules. Where only a few ferns are grown in pots, regular liquid feeding through the growing months may be more convenient. Allow tree fern trunks to root well into the compost before supplying any feed.

Using ferns

Ferns, being predominently shade-loving, mix well with many woodland herbaceous perennials. Various species of toad lily (*Trillium*) are beautiful companions, as are the Martagon lily (*Lilium martagon*) and similar lily species. dog's-tooth violet (*Erythronium*) is another favourite, while the snowdrop (*Galanthus*) in all its many forms and species is unsurpassable, looking particularly good with *Polypodium australe* and its cultivars, as both are at their peak in late winter. In fact, virtually all woodland bulbous plants are suitable, especially those that emerge early in the season, before the new fern fronds unfurl.

On the downside, the persistence and post-flowering elongation of the leaves of bulbs such as snowdrops is not always welcome. Hellebores come into the same category – beautiful when they flower but with overpowering summer foliage unless plenty of space is allowed.

Hostas are excellent and popular candidates for mixed plantings, especially with the feathery forms of dryopteris and polystichum. They are not so good with the glossy leathery fronds of hart's tongue fern (*Asplenium scolopendrium*), however, as their foliage is rather too similar.

Ferns are beautiful with grasses and bamboos (not the invasive kinds). At Burford House gardens in Shropshire I have seen various grasses planted with *Polystichum setiferum* 'Plumosum Bevis' and *P. setiferum* 'Plumoso-multilobum' and was very impressed at how well the two types of plants complemented each other.

In damper areas where larger ferns like osmunda are being grown, candelabra primulas, *Gunnera manicata*, irises and other water-margin plants are perfect natural partners. The projects on pp.86–114 contain some more ideas for using ferns in the garden.

Stumperies and rockeries

There is a place for both stumperies and rockeries in modern gardens. Rockeries make an excellent backdrop for mountain plants, while stumperies come into their own in a woodland setting. Many ferns can be classed as alpines, that is small enough to be kept in small greenhouses or grown on rockeries and as such they look wonderful with a range of alpine plants. Among my favourites are lewisias, saxifrages and primulas.

The concept of stumperies was promoted in the nineteenth century, particularly as a setting for ferns and as an alternative to a rockery where rock was not obtainable. Basically, it was suggested that tree stumps with a length of trunk still attached should be planted upside down in the ground

Left: A cyclamen grows through *Polypodium vulgare* 'Jean Taylor'.

Ferns look wonderful displayed among the decaying remains of tree stumps and trunks.

with the root mass looking like a small dead shrub. When I first came across this idea I thought it sounded unattractive and I dismissed it as being not to my taste. Subsequently, I exhibited ferns at many flower shows, and, presented with the problem of how to hide the plant pots, resorted to using old stumps and branches, with great success. I now use the wood, even if it is not essential for cover. I love the way the various shades of brown and the rough shapes of the wood set off the greens and delicate forms of the ferns.

It is very easy to develop a stumpery in the garden. Make an apparently haphazard arrangement of irregularly shaped pieces of wood or tree stumps and plant the ferns in between. The larger the pieces of wood the better; slender branches are not so effective.

Groundcover

The majority of ferns have erect rhizomes that stay where you put them, but a few do have spreading rhizomes or stolons and are able to colonize quite large areas. Most spreading ferns are deciduous. The polypodiums are the exception and are probably the best candidates for groundcover in most situations. Speed up their spread by cutting a clump into many small pieces and planting them out 15cm (6in) apart. In a couple of seasons the pieces should have joined up, rapidly increasing the clump size.

If a larger clump is required, the operation can be repeated again, and again. It is as well not to plant different polypodiums close to each other as in time they become intertwined and then difficult to separate.

Other notable examples of spreading ferns are: *Gymnocarpium dryopteris*, *Matteuccia struthiopteris*, *Onoclea sensibilis*, *Phegopteris connectilis* and *Thelypteris palustris*.

Matteuccia struthiopteris spreads by stolons. The rhizomes are erect, in time making each crown into a small tree fern. New crowns appear at random. If they grow where they are not wanted, they are easily removed and can then be given away, swapped or otherwise disposed of.

Onoclea sensibilis and *Thelypteris palustris* both spread quite rapidly but the rhizomes are near the surface so their spread is usually fairly easily kept in check. *Gymnocarpium dryopteris* also spreads near the surface but can become difficult to eradicate if allowed to become entangled with other plants. It has colonized large areas at Hergest Croft gardens near Kington in Herefordshire where it looks beautiful. Other species of gymnocarpium spread in much the same way, as does *Phegopteris connectilis*.

Onoclea sensibilis makes good ground-cover, especially beside watercourses and pools.

Tree ferns

A tree fern is more or less like any other fern with large fronds, except that, in time, it produces a trunk, which may eventually reach 18m (60ft) tall. The trunk consists of a central caudex (a hardy woody stem with conducting tissue) surrounded by a mass of old leaf bases, fibre and roots.

There are over 600 different species of tree fern. Although most are in the genus *Cyathea* (split by some experts into a number of smaller genera including *Cnemidaria* and *Sphaeropteris*), the most widely grown in cultivation are species from the relatively small genus *Dicksonia*, particularly *Dicksonia antarctica*. *Cibotium* and *Lophosoria* are two other small, related genera. Species from some other genera, notably *Blechnum* also produce trunks, but they are not true tree ferns. *Dryopteris affinis* may grow a stump a few centimetres high. Unfortunately, as the stump gets taller with age, the roots dry out and the plant eventually dies.

Horticulturally, *Dicksonia antarctica* has many advantages over almost all the other tree fern species. It is nearly hardy in the cool temperate climates, such as that of the British Isles. It is incredibly easy to grow. It is able to live through being shipped from Australia, which takes seven weeks in a container. Most remarkable of all, it can survive being sawn off at ground level as a mature tree up to 6m (20ft) in height. The severed plant has no roots apart from those on the trunk. When, in due course, the trunk is planted on the other side of the world, it produces new fronds in 4–6 weeks and within a year has rooted into its new growing medium! The survival rate with the thousands of trunks I imported to my nursery was something like 99 percent, and the failures were down to mistakes by the growers over here. How many other trees would survive such abuse?

Many other tree fern species are listed in A–Z of Ferns (pp.25–85) but none has been proven to withstand this treatment. *Dicksonia squarrosa* is a possibility as it sometimes grows when the severed trunks are used as fence posts in its native New Zealand, but only a smallish proportion of these trunks produce fronds, and I suspect even fewer become properly established.

Which tree fern?

For those in cool temperate regions who have never grown a tree fern before, *Dicksonia antarctica* is the first choice. It is tough, relatively hardy and has been in cultivation long enough for a fair bit to be known about what it will or will not tolerate. There are two other species that can do well outdoors in zone 8. The first is *Dicksonia fibrosa*. When well protected I have known it to survive temperatures of

In the appropriate setting, tree ferns are truly spectacular. Right: *Dicksonia antarctica*; far right: *Dicksonia squarrosa*.

−12°C (10°F). However, it is superficially very similar to *D. antarctica* although it seems to grow faster; for something quite different I recommend *Cyathea australis*. It comes from the same general area of Australia, but it is found in more open places and should, therefore, stand exposure and frost better. Its altitude limit is very similar to *D. antarctica* and may even go slightly higher, another plus factor. Overall, it may prove to be at least as hardy as *D. antarctica*. On the debit side it is apparently deciduous, even in Australia, whereas *D. antarctica* is often evergreen.

For anyone lucky enough to live in an area where frosts are rare, there are other species that can be considered. I have heard of plants of *Cyathea dealbata*, *C. smithii*, *Dicksonia squarrosa* and *D. sellowiana* doing well. *D. sellowiana* may prove to be as hardy as *D. antarctica* but information is currently limited.

Light filtering through the airy fronds of Dicksonia sellowiana.

Cultivating *Dicksonia antarctica*

If the specimen is purchased as a log, soak the base of the trunk for a few minutes prior to planting. If it is to be planted out in the garden, select a shady spot, out of the wind; in less suitable conditions the plant tends to produce shorter fronds. Plant the log so that as little as possible is buried, while ensuring that it will not topple

over. (As tree ferns are normally priced according to the length of trunk, burying unnecessary trunk is effectively burying money.) Once the trunk is firmly in position, water it copiously. I direct the full force of a hose all over and all around the trunk, from about 10cm (4in) below the top down to ground level. Some growers advocate filling the crown with water; I am not keen on this practice, particularly if the weather is cold and damp, when the crown might remain uncomfortably wet for some time, perhaps encouraging rot.

Keep the log watered daily if possible, especially in more exposed sites, until the new leaves have emerged and expanded. Missing the odd day is not serious, but a well-watered plant produces longer fronds and is generally better set up for the next season, too. My long-established plants are not so good now as they were when they were tended and watered daily. They are still attractive but the fronds are now only 1.5–2m (5–6ft) long instead of 2.5m (9ft). I do not normally feed my dicksonias in the garden. They seem to manage with plenty of water and the basic soil nutrients.

To grow a tree fern in a pot, again, plant the log as shallowly as possible. Water copiously and within six months the log should have rooted and become secure. Use a pot as small as possible for the log at first. There are several reasons for this: because the plant needs to be watered so much over the first few months, the soil inevitably gets very wet and a smaller pot has a better chance of drying out a little between waterings; the unrooted log is very difficult to secure in a large pot unless it is planted unacceptably deep; and smaller pots are easier to move around and are more economical on composts.

After one full year in the small pot (normally the next spring), the plant should have produced roots that will be appearing out of the drainage holes. When this happens it is time to pot it on. At this stage I feed my plants for the first time. I avoid feeding for the first year as I want the log to root into the compost. If it is fed too much nitrogen, there is a risk that a lot of foliage will be produced with little or no root, possibly stressing the plant if it is allowed to dry out at all. (Feeding with a high potash/low nitrogen product to encourage root growth may be fine but in my experience is not necessary.) Once roots are evident I am happy to feed with a general-purpose fertilizer.

Most tree ferns need much the same cultivation techniques as for *D. antarctica*, except that many are far less hardy and need to be kept under glass in cool climates (see Winter care).

A pair of specimens of *Cyathea dealbata*, looking entirely at home in County Kerry, Ireland.

Cyathea smithii has abundant brown scales, enhancing its stipes.

Winter care

Unfortunately no tree fern is totally hardy in the temperatures experienced by most of the British Isles (zone 8). Recent winters have been very mild and virtually all *Dicksonia antarctica* have thrived outdoors, whether protected or not. However, please do not be lulled into a feeling of false security. Hard winters can be a problem and very hard winters fatal unless sensible precautions are taken.

The safest way to grow tree ferns is to keep them all in a conservatory all year round. In a sunny conservatory they must be watered abundantly in hot weather during the growing period. They also need water from time to time in winter, especially if the conservatory is heated. In a shady conservatory, management is easier but plenty of water is still needed. In Britain *Cyathea australis*, *Dicksonia antarctica* and *D. fibrosa* should not need any heat over winter. Some other species, including *Cyathea dealbata*, *C. dregei*, *C. smithii* and *Dicksonia squarrosa* and most of the other tree ferns in A–Z of Ferns (pp.25–85) prefer the minimum temperature to be at or above freezing.

Cyathea australis, *Dicksonia antarctica* and *D. fibrosa* may also be grown outdoors on a patio or plunged in pots into the garden from spring to autumn and then moved inside into a protected environment for winter. This is especially important for smaller plants, around 60cm (2ft), which are less hardy than taller ones. Fortunately, they are also lighter and not too difficult to move around.

Larger plants of the three hardiest species can be left out over winter but need protecting in zone 8 or colder. It seems to me that it is the meristem (the bud tissue in the crown) that is vital for the continued success of the plant, so from late October (the end of the growing season) to mid-April I protect this area.

The ring of fronds at the top of the trunk forms a funnel that leads down into the trunk very nearly as low as the meristem.

New fronds of *Dicksonia antarctica*.

This funnel will readily collect water. To prevent this from happening I stuff it with straw to about 15cm (6in) above the top of the trunk. This keeps the meristem warmer and excludes the worst of the winter wet, greatly reducing the risk of a block of ice forming in the crown. In a mild winter this is sufficient protection for large plants of 1.2m (4ft) or taller. For shorter plants, in addition to the straw I wrap an insulating material around the top of the trunk. I use a belt of polystyrene plant trays, tied together and cushioned from the trunk with more straw – the straw is stuffed behind the trays and keeps them secure. I also tie a circular piece of polystyrene over the crown, which helps divert rainwater away from the meristem. In this way the top of the trunk is fully boxed in against the cold, and to some extent the wet. If particularly severe weather is forecast, further layers of insulation, perhaps sacking or straw bales, can be positioned around the trunk. In places that rarely experience frosts, protection such as this is less likely to be necessary.

Many people use garden fleece instead of polystyrene for protection, but as recent winters have been very mild I remain cautious. Another favourite material is bubble wrap, but I think it could lead to the crown sweating and then possibly rotting. I have heard of tops of tree ferns being completely wrapped in polythene, leaves and all. Again, this could create the ideal breeding ground for rots.

Environmental impact

Some concern has been expressed over the wholesale harvest of tree ferns from the forests of Australia (and New Zealand). However, when I visited the harvesting sites in the Otway Ranges to the south-west of Melbourne I became convinced that tree fern harvesting from the wild is sustainable and is having no significant environmental effect. Forestry is the main industry in the tree fern areas. When areas of eucalyptus forest are felled for timber, all plants in the understories are bulldozed and burned. The areas are immediately reseeded with forestry trees. Eucalyptus forests are harvested every 60 or so years, giving *D. antarctica* and *C. australis* (below) plenty of time to recolonize. In addition, during felling some areas remain untouched. State laws insist that all waterways have an undamaged buffer zone either side; even for damp ditches this is something like 50m (160ft). These fingers of virgin forest make it easier for the natural forest species to merge into the commercial forest.

Those who harvest tree ferns are salvaging a waste product of the timber industry. They are given little notice of where the next felling operation will take place and must get in to the designated area (not easy as the forests are usually trackless) and remove as many of the tree ferns as possible in a short time. Of course, not all the tree ferns can be salvaged. For example, laws forbid removal of *Cyathea cunninghamii*, even though the forestry activities will destroy specimens in the way. It is important to reiterate that forestry is vital for the local population and that the foresters are only doing their job. But it remains that tree fern harvesting really is a salvage operation with no environmental impact in itself.

Propagation

Growing ferns from spores can take a long time but it is the best method of propagation and should result in plenty of new plants. (To fully understand propagation by spores it is useful to know about a fern's lifecycle, see p.120; technical terms are explained in the glossary, p.119.)

The first step is to collect your spores. For most species, this is best done in midsummer. To select ripe spores, examine the sori on the underside of the frond: if the sporangia are exposed, glossy, dark brown or black, they are probably ripe; if they look rough or shaggy, they have probably already shed their spores and all you can see is the broken sporangia walls; if they are green or only pale brown, they are probably not ripe. Spores normally ripen in sequence from the base to the tip of the frond, therefore you can often find ripe and unripe spores on a single frond.

When you have found a section of the frond with ripe spores, break off a small piece, perhaps a pinna, and put it in an envelope. Leave this in a dry place for 48 hours, then tap the envelope vigorously and a very fine dust should appear at the bottom of the envelope. Check whether you have spores or just rubbish by examining the dust with a good hand lens. Spores will appear as thousands of specks mostly of identical size. Spores can be stored, but germination is much better if they are sown sooner rather than later.

Next, wash your pots and fill them with compost. Ericaceous compost with a low nutrient content or peat give good results. The compost needs to be sterilized to prevent the emerging ferns (prothalli) from being swamped by fungi, bacteria, mosses or liverworts. Do this by pouring boiling water over it, scalding the surface. Place the treated pots in a clean polythene bag, seal it and leave to cool. The next day sprinkle your spores onto the sterile surface, label the pots, return them to the polythene

The green spores of *Matteuccia struthiopteris* should be sown as soon as they are collected. Large clumps of this fern are also easily propagated by division.

bag and reseal. Ensure you do the sowing in a still atmosphere. Store the pots in good light but not direct sun; they will not need watering.

If the spores are sown in midsummer, a film of green should be seen over the surface of the compost within a month or two; the first true fronds may be produced before the onset of winter, but it is more likely they will appear the following spring. Autumn sowings take much longer to develop. Once sufficient true fronds have been produced, remove the pots from the polythene bag, place them in indirect light, and lightly lay the polythene bag over the top; water the surface very carefully as necessary. This is a way of hardening-off the young plants: immediate exposure to dry air can be fatal.

Gradually expose the young ferns to the open air and, when you are satisfied they are tough enough, prick out the little plants into seed trays that have been surface-sterilized 24 hours beforehand. Prick out in clumps so there is a good chance that at least some young plants' roots will survive the operation. Place a polythene sheet over the freshly pricked-out ferns for a few days to help prevent drying out until their root systems have recovered. Once they have been hardened-off, the plants should grow away strongly and can be potted-on into plugs or individual pots.

Some ferns have green spores when ripe, notably *Osmunda* and *Lygodium*. Their spores tend to be ripe in mid- to late summer. *Matteuccia struthiopteris* and *Onoclea sensibilis* also have green spores but they are shed in midwinter. All green spores need to be sown as soon as possible after collection; they are only viable for about two weeks under normal conditions. Although not green, tree fern spores also tend to be shortlived and should also be sown within a fortnight of collection. If immediate sowing is not possible, spores can be stored for longer if kept cool: the top of a fridge is suitable.

Division

Once a fern with a creeping rhizome has produced at least two growing tips, the parts can be separated with a sharp knife and planted out separately. In practice, it is best to split a good-sized colony. This can then be cut into small parts without worrying about whether or not there is a growing point on each.

Splitting a main crown is a simple but very slow way to build up stocks. It is the only way to reproduce some sterile cultivars and because spore-produced progeny are not necessarily the same as their parent, dividing the main crown can be a useful way of propagating fertile cultivars. Unfortunately, some species remain as single crowns throughout their lives.

The splitting process can be carried out with a knife or, with large clumps, two forks. I prefer the latter. Select the line where the division is to be made, insert one fork vertically along this line, then insert the other fork in the same line but with its back to the first fork so that the two handles are

Ferns to propagate by division

Athyrium, creeping varieties
Gymnocarpium
Matteuccia struthiopteris
Onoclea sensibilis
Phegopteris connectilis
Polypodium
Pyrrosia sheareri (below)
Other rhizomatous ferns

leaning away from each other. Bring the two handles together gently to push apart the two sections of rhizome. Repeat on the fragments as required. Large splits can be planted straight into the garden but small pieces are best potted up and grown on first.

Bulbils

Quite a few ferns produce bulbils on their fronds. With care these can be grown on into new plants. All offspring should be identical to the parent, but there are rare exceptions, so it is worth keeping an eye open for breaks.

Bulbils are produced most commonly on cultivars of *Polystichum setiferum*, such

Polystichum setiferum 'Multilobum' produces bulbils on its fronds and these can be used for propagation.

as 'Divisilobum', 'Plumoso-divisilobum', 'Cristato-pinnulum', 'Multilobum' and others. Other species of *Polystichum*, including *P. andersonii* and *P. proliferum*, and *Woodwardia unigemmata* also produce one or two bulbils near the tip of the frond. In some species of *Cystopteris*, such as *C. bulbifera*, bulbils are produced along the underside of the rachis. These fall off and grow happily without any connection to the parent plant.

Some cultivars of *Athyrium filix-femina*, for example 'Plumosum Superbum Dissectum Druery' and 'Clarissima', produce bulbils as replacements for sporangia in the indusia, or elsewhere on the frond. They are difficult to see even with a lens, but if a mature frond is laid down (see below) young plantlets can be raised quite easily. Ferns produced from bulbils on 'Clarissima' are likely to be inferior to the original. This form of reproduction is a type of apospory.

Grow bulbils by following this procedure. Fill a seed tray with peat. Scrape a shallow groove in the peat, then sterilize the surface with boiling water. Allow to cool. Select a frond with ripe bulbils (usually already with conspicuous small frondlets), lay it in the groove and anchor it firmly in position by either pegging it to the peat or sprinkling grit lightly over it. Water it and then lay a polythene sheet loosely over the tray to help control water loss. Keeping an eye on the watering, leave the frond undisturbed in a greenhouse or coldframe for a few months (with *Athyrium filix-femina* cultivars keep the bulbils frost free because the parent frond is deciduous). Usually by the following spring there are obvious rows of little plantlets and these can be carefully teased out of the tray and potted up in a low nutrient mix, which forces the bulbils to produce roots.

Leaf base bulbils

Leaf base bulbils are a useful way of propagating the sterile cultivars of *Asplenium scolopendrium*, such as 'Crispum'. Select the mature parent. Dig it up and wash off all the soil. Low down

When mature, specimens of *Asplenium scolopendrium* 'Crispum' can yield up to a hundred new plants when propagated using leaf base bulbils.

in the clump there will be old sections of rhizome covered with short, dead-looking leaf bases. Peel these downwards, oldest first, so that they break off cleanly; they are green at the point of attachment, but no bulbil is normally visible. Take only as many as you require; do not collect the bases of green fronds, as these will not be mature and they are still doing a job for the plant. Keep the detached leaf bases in a polythene bag until you are ready to continue. Replant the parent, giving it some tender loving care until it has recovered.

Wash the leaf bases, cleaning off remnants of old frond and any root material. Prepare a pot or tray of sand or low-nutrient compost. Surface sterilize it with boiling water. Allow to cool. Plant the leaf bases upside down, with the cut end (the point of attachment to the parent) facing upwards. Space them about a centimetre (½in) apart. Place the pot or tray into a new or very clean polythene bag and place it on a windowsill in good indirect light.

In one or two months there should be a green swelling (or more) on the tip of each base: the bulbil. After a few more months, little fronds will appear and once little plantlets are formed and are about 1–2cm (½in) tall, the plastic bag can be removed. A day or two afterwards the plantlets can be pricked out. Harden them off just as with all small ferns.

Pests and diseases

As long as they are grown in the right conditions – plenty of moisture and shade and humus-rich soil – ferns suffer few health problems.

Fortunately ferns suffer from few problems. What diseases there are can often be eliminated or at least kept in check by good husbandry. Most importantly this involves cutting off all old fronds before the new ones unfurl, when it is a quick, easy job. Removing old fronds breaks the cycle of disease and limits lasting damage. It also has the advantage of keeping the plants looking tidy. In addition, avoid watering fronds: water straight to the roots wherever possible, not to the crown, just in case there are any rots around. (This also applies to tree ferns, see pp.14–17 for more information on growing them.)

The two most serious rots are *Milesina scolopendri* on *Asplenium scolopendrium* and *Taphrina wettsteiniana* on *Polystichum setiferum* and related species of *Polystichum* (see relevant entries in A–Z of Ferns, pp.25–85). The old fronds of polystichums, particularly the densely foliose forms, such as *P. setiferum* 'Plumoso-multilobum', can be disfigured at the base by a black rot, possibly a species of *Rhizoctonia* or *Botrytis*. Again, avoid wetting the crown during watering. If the rot develops in the garden, either spray with a systemic fungicide or clear all debris away from the crown to facilitate good air circulation.

Greenfly, blackfly and capsids

Greenfly and blackfly are rare on ferns in the garden; they are more likely to occur on plants grown indoors in the house or greenhouse.

If spraying is unavoidable, soapy water can be tried, but I have little confidence in it. I use a pyrethroid insecticide, at half dose, when necessary. To avoid scorching, spray in the evening when there is no risk of the sun burning the damp fronds. One pest that seems to be controlled only by spraying is capsid, which grazes the frond creating tiny white blotches at random. Capsids are not often a real worry unless the ferns are being prepared for show – then, of course, any insecticide scorch is doubly undesirable.

Slugs and snails

Slugs and snails are very rarely attracted to ferns. The most notable exceptions are some of the thicker-textured fronds found among the spleenworts (*Asplenium*). Whenever they do become a nuisance try sharp grit around the plant or, failing that, resort to slug pellets. In my polytunnels I find frogs are quite an effective means of control!

Vine weevil

Vine weevil grubs are a common pest, their grubs eating any part of the plant, usually starting with the roots and moving on to the leaf bases. Vine weevil is common in gardens, but rarely causes any problems outdoors: it is with pot-grown plants that the real damage is done. Certain ferns are more susceptible than others. With me, *Asplenium scolopendrium* is the worst affected, but in bad years, following mild winters, others can be attacked.

The first visible symptoms are plants wilting while their soil is moist so it is obvious that drought is not the problem. Gently pull the fronds: if they come away easily, vine weevil is almost certainly the cause. Tip the remains of the plant out of the pot and sift through the compost. Look for white banana-shaped grubs, anything up to 5mm (¼in) long. These may be anywhere in the pot but particularly among the remains of the crown. If you have caught them early, the weevils may not have caused irretrievable damage. Remove it immediately and repot it. However, recovery is usually a long process and I do not usually try to resuscitate weeviled plants unless the damaged fern is something rather special.

Unfortunately, weevil damage is not confined to

A healthy selection of ferns, flourishing in damp conditions.

grubs eating the parts under the soil; the adult weevils nibble at the margins of fronds, leaving otherwise straight margins irritatingly scalloped. Fortunately, this is not too serious to the health of the plant, but is a nuisance if they are being grown for showing. The adults are easily recognized. They are black crawling insects with a long pointed snout. They are more readily found at night and if seen should be crushed.

Control of weevils is not easy, especially as many chemical controls have been withdrawn from the market. There is a nematode that parasitizes weevils, which can be added to the compost. I have never used it but I have heard mixed reports. I suggest regular inspection of the root ball together with night-time torchlight sessions in the greenhouse. Alternatively, try to avoid the problem by planting out *Asplenium scolopendrium* and other susceptible species.

Eelworm

Typically eelworm damage is seen as dead patches of frond confined by larger veins. Control is just about impossible. It is best to remove fronds suspected of being infected as soon as possible. The problem is most likely in damp, humid conditions.

Parts of a fern

A typical fern leaf (frond) consists of a stem (stipe) and leafy portion (lamina), supported on a midrib (rachis) which can branch. Fern fronds can be various basic shapes.

The anatomy of a fern

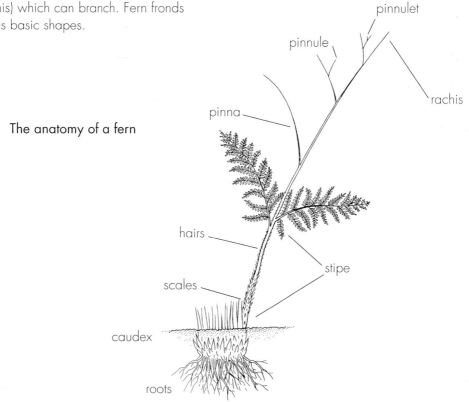

pinnulet

pinnule

rachis

pinna

hairs

stipe

scales

caudex

roots

Fern frond shapes

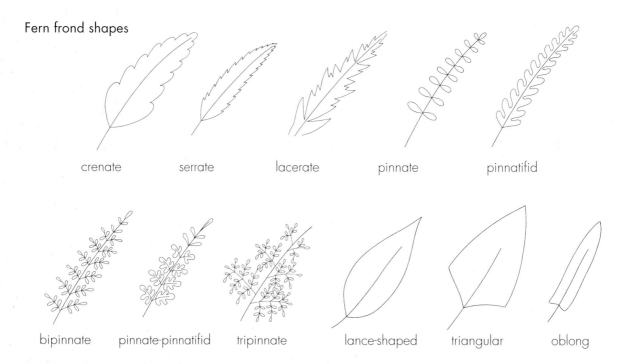

crenate   serrate   lacerate   pinnate   pinnatifid

bipinnate   pinnate-pinnatifid   tripinnate   lance-shaped   triangular   oblong

A–Z
of Ferns

This chapter includes ferns that are good garden
plants, or cold greenhouse plants in cool temperate
regions. The majority have either been grown in
my garden in central England or in my unheated
polytunnels. Although some may need protection,
they are worth growing because they are
especially interesting.

Key

✱ Frond length, sometimes also frond width; affected by growing conditions.

🍃 Deciduous: more or less disappears over winter.

Evergreen: green all year, but may look tatty by spring.

Wintergreen: green most of the winter but usually tatty by midwinter, except *Polypodium australe* and its cultivars, which send up new fronds in mid- to late summer and die down in mid- to late spring.

Z The coldest hardiness zone each species is likely to survive in, although experimentation is often worthwhile; some protection overwinter is usually advisable. (For more information, see pp.116–17.)

≈ Dry/Wet: needs a well-drained site in shade.

Wet/Dry: needs a mostly damp site in shade.

Wet: best beside water or in a bog; will tolerate full sun as long as water is plentiful.

🌐 Country or continent of origin.

At the end of its description, each fern is given an availability rating. Rare: sometimes available from specialized nurseries; quite rare: usually available from specialized nurseries; quite common: sometimes available at garden centres; common: usually available at garden centres.

Adiantum Maidenhair ferns

Distributed worldwide.

This is one of the most beautiful of all the fern genera. It is a huge genus with, unfortunately, only relatively few hardy or half hardy species. All species listed are worth acquiring, and a little trouble taken to protect half hardy species can be very rewarding. No doubt, in time, more hardy species suitable for sheltered niches, even in quite cold gardens, will be discovered. Maidenhair ferns are very distinctive. The pinnules are borne on thin, shiny black stems. The pinnae themselves are usually oblong or fan-shaped. Characteristically the spores are produced in a sorus formed by a fold along the distal edge of the pinnule. Maidenhair ferns are not normally fussy about soil type; certainly many species actually prefer lime.

↕ 30–60cm / 12–24in

▨ Deciduous

Z 3

≈≈ Dry/Wet, avoid windy sites

⊕ Western coast of North America, Japan.

A. aleuticum AGM

Aleutian maidenhair

Fronds pale green, pedate (erect stipe divides into a fan of finger-like sections), each 'finger' further divided into a series of triangular segments (pinnules). Eventually forms a clump. Like 'Japonicum' (below) new fronds are occasionally slightly flushed with pink. This is such a deservedly popular fern that various wild collections have been named unofficially. For example "Patrick Creek" and "Perry Creek" are both attractive plants but not sufficiently distinct to warrant varietal status. Quite common. (*A. pedatum*, p.28, is very similar to *A. aleuticum*.)

Adiantum aleuticum

Adiantum aleuticum 'Subpumilum'

'Imbricatum', 15–30cm (6–12in), is intermediate between the typical plant and 'Subpumilum'. Comes more or less true from spores. '**Japonicum**' (Japanese maidenhair), 30–45cm (12–18in), zone 8, is sometimes referred to as "Asiatic forms". It differs from the typical plant by having rosy-pink foliage with contrasting black stipes in spring. There is some doubt over whether this is correctly placed under *A. aleuticum* or *A. pedatum*. Originating from the Pacific fringes, it is remote from the east coast of North America, and therefore more logically allied to *A. aleuticum*, but curiously there is sometimes a relationship between the floras of Japan and the east coast of America. DNA analysis in the future will reveal its true identity. This form is less reliable in the garden: it seems to need more shelter and is probably less hardy. '**Subpumilum**' AGM (dwarf maidenhair), 7–15cm (3–6in), deciduous, wintergreen in a mild winter, has overlapping pinnae and is more tolerant of wind. Ideal for borders, stone troughs or rock gardens. In the wild this form is rare, only known from a handful of sites in the Pacific north-west of America. It grows in proximity to the typical plant along with plants of all intermediate sizes, see 'Imbricatum'. In horticulture it, nevertheless, comes true from spores.

↕ 30–38cm/12–15in

▨ Deciduous

Z 9, possibly 8

≋ Dry/Wet

⊕ Worldwide

A. capillus-veneris

True maidenhair

Fronds bipinnate, each pinnule rounded with a crenate margin on sterile fronds. If fertile, the sori are formed from the reflexed edge of pinnules. Typically the sorus is elongated, not circular. (The very similar tender species *A. cuneatum* has circular sori.) The only British native maidenhair, this species is found in many parts of the world. In Britain it is a maritime species recorded from a few sites along the south and west coasts, plus some inland sites on sheltered walls. In the wild the plant luxuriates in areas where water runs over lime-bearing rock; tufa is often formed on site. The running water may help to protect against low winter temperatures; despite the frequent presence of running water the plants are never waterlogged. Not reliably hardy in central Britain, it succeeded for me in a sheltered, well-drained site, although the fronds were very small and late in appearing. During the nineteenth century many cultivars were in cultivation. However, many were only slightly different from the parent type and most are now extinct. Quite rare.

↕ 38cm/15in

▨ Deciduous

Z 8

≋ Dry

A. x mairisii AGM

Mairis's hybrid maidenhair

Fronds bipinnate with rounded pinnules on a shiny black rachis and midrib. This hybrid fern was raised at the nursery of Mairis and Co before 1885. It was named by Thomas Moore, who thought the parentage might be *A. capillus-veneris* and *A. cuneatum*. Over a hundred years later this parentage still seems possible as modern chromosome counts are consistent with Moore's theory. The fern resembles *A. capillus-veneris* in general form but is more erect with slightly smaller pinnules and has greater vigour; it is, therefore, a far better garden plant. Its greatest asset is its hardiness – I have grown it outdoors for decades; my only concession to slight tenderness is to plant it among stones. In time it spreads beyond any protection and thrives. It remains rare in cultivation, but it has a spreading habit and can be divided periodically to increase stock. Rare.

↕ 45–60cm/18–24in

▨ Deciduous

Z 3, avoid windy sites

≋ Dry

⊕ Eastern North America

A. pedatum AGM

Eastern maidenhair

True *A. pedatum* is very uncommon in cultivation, at least in Europe; plants supplied as *A. pedatum* are usually *A. aleuticum*. It is difficult to define the differences between the two as both have pedate fronds with shiny black-brown rachis and midribs, but mature plants seen side by side are clearly different. As a guide, *A. pedatum* has larger pinnules with rounded crenulate lobes; each pinnule is held in the same plane as the frond, ie. flat. In *A. aleuticum* the pinnules are smaller with angular denticulate lobes and each pinnule is twisted out of the plane of the frond. In *A. pedatum* each frond has more branches, and is usually a paler green. In a well-lit site the fronds of *A. pedatum* arch laxly while those of *A. aleuticum* tend to be more stiffly erect. At shows where both species are on display *A. pedatum* wins in terms of general appreciation. Propagate by spores. Quite rare.

Asiatic forms, 30–45cm (12–18in), are sometimes sold. New fronds are pink. Plants I have seen are forms of *A. aleuticum* 'Japonicum'. **'Miss Sharples'**, 30–45cm (12–18in), was given to the well-known nurseryman Reginald Kaye many years ago by a Miss Sharples. He simply labelled it 'Miss Sharples' so he could remember its provenance. Unknown to him another nurseryman collected spores,

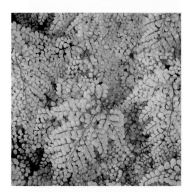

Adiantum venustum

↕ 22–38cm/9–15in

🍃 Deciduous, sometimes wintergreen

Z 5

≈ Dry

🌐 Central Asia

assumed 'Miss Sharples' was its correct name and sold plants under that name. The name has stuck. Until recently I thought 'Miss Sharples' was a form of *A. aleuticum*. However, at the time it appeared and before, the North American maidenhair fern offered by British nurseries was probably exclusively *A. pedatum*. (*A. aleuticum* was introduced more recently – possibly by Judith Jones, proprietor of the nursery Fancy Fronds in Seattle.) This and the fact that it has much larger pinnules and a paler frond colour, suggests that it is a form of *A. pedatum*. It differs from the type plant in having conspicuously lobed pinnules.

A. venustum AGM
Himalayan maidenhair
Croziers of new fronds are pink. They emerge in early spring and withstand late frosts with ease. Fronds rapidly turn dull green. Rhizomes creep near soil surface and produce tripinnate, narrowly triangular fronds. Gradually spreads to give excellent groundcover in dryish to moist shade or semi-shade. Best propagated by division but ensure sections of rhizome are not buried too deeply and that they are firmly fixed – freshly planted-out rhizomes of *A. venustum* make excellent bird-nesting material. Quite rare.

Arachniodes

Widespread throughout northern temperate zones.
An attractive genus closely related to *Polystichum* and *Dryopteris*. The sorus is kidney-shaped, as in *Dryopteris*, but the pinnules terminate in bristles and the frond texture is often leathery, rather like *Polystichum*. There are many species other than that listed here. They are not in general cultivation but could be well worth trying. Some species were formerly placed in *Leptorumohra* or *Polystichopsis*.

Arachniodes standishii

↕ 45–60cm/18–24in

🍃 Wintergreen

Z 5

≈ Dry/Wet

🌐 Japan, Korea

A. standishii formerly *Polystichopsis standishii*
Upside-down fern
Fronds ovate, tripinnate, pale green. Spores produced mainly towards base of frond. The ovate frond is quite different from most members of the genus. Rare.

Asplenium

Worldwide.
Asplenium is a very large genus with plants greatly varying appearance and greatly differing cultural requirements. All species have a rather leathery feel to the fronds and all have elongated sori. This list includes a selection of species; many others are known but they are either of little garden merit or very similar in appearance to included species. *A. scolopendrium* has in the past been placed in its own genus, *Phyllitis*, but modern concensus has sunk it into *Asplenium*. Culturally it is easier to grow than most small asplenia from temperate regions. Tropical and warm temperate species are not included here.

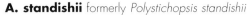

↕ 7–38m/3–15in

🌢 Evergreen

Z 4

≈ Dry/Wet

🌐 Europe, including British Isles, Asia, North America

↕ 7–10cm (3–4in)

🌢 Evergreen

Z 5

≈ Dry/Wet

🌐 South America

↕ 15–20cm/6–8in

🌢 Evergreen

Z 6

≈ Dry/Wet

🌐 Eastern USA

↕ 12–38cm/5–15in

🌢 Evergreen

Z 5

≈ Dry/Wet

🌐 North America

↕ 45–60cm/18–24in

🌢 Evergreen

Z 5

≈ Dry/Wet

🌐 Europe, including British Isles

A. adiantum-nigrum

Black spleenwort

Fronds leathery, triangular, bi- to tripinnate. The common name is derived from the black rachis – particularly on the underside. Difficult to cultivate in pots as it is easily overwatered, but usually easy in the garden if given good drainage. Rare.

A. dareoides

Fronds tripinnate and roundly triangular with slightly rounded segments. A beautiful creeping fern, easily grown in a shady border with good drainage. Rare.

A. x ebenoides

A fertile hybrid (*A. platyneuron* x *A. rhizophyllus*). Fronds suberect, pinnate with variable shaped pinnae, usually triangular. Will root from the tip of some leaves. Quite intermediate between the parents. Cultivate in a well-drained site or an alpine house. Rare.

A. platyneuron

Ebony spleenwort

Fronds pinnate with dark brown rachis. Sterile fronds spreading, fertile fronds more erect. Pinnae narrowly triangular and alternate along the rachis. Superficially similar to *A. trichomanes* but pinnae shape and growth form is distinctive. Tolerant of a wide range of pH but must have good drainage. Rare.

A. scolopendrium AGM,

syn. *Phyllitis scolopendrium*, *Scolopendrium vulgare*

Hart's tongue fern

Fronds strap-shaped, entire. Clump-forming, excellent as a contrast to the more feathery types of fern. Prefers lime in soil; this is not essential but plants are less luxuriant in very acid conditions. Best in full or semi-shade as bright midday sun can burn brown lesions into the fronds. There are related species around the northern hemisphere. Occasionally in wet seasons or in particularly wet sites, the fungus disease *Milesina scolopendrii* can infect fronds. The symptoms are brown lesions, not unlike sunburn, but they differ in producing a few

Asplenium scolopendrium

white powdery spores in the centre of the lesion on the lower surface. The disease can be kept in check by removing infected fronds and by cleaning up established plants in the spring just before the new fronds emerge. If preferred, a rust-active systemic fungicide may be applied. In North America, var. *americanum* looks similar (it has half the number of chromosomes) but it is not such a strong grower; *A. lindenii* from Mexico may be the same taxon. *Phyllitis* (*Asplenium*) *japonicum* looks similar but may be genetically distinct. The robust character of the European hart's tongue fern makes it one of the very best garden plants. Common.

Asplenium scolopendrium
'Crispum'

Fortunately there are many cultivars in cultivation. All are fertile, except the best forms of 'Crispum', and all are worth growing. **Crispum Group**, 30–60cm (12–24in). Fronds sterile, green and deeply goffered – from the side they resemble an Elizabethan ruff. The Crispum Group of cultivars are the plumose form (see p.118) and the cream of the hart's tongues. Being sterile they are rarely propagated, but may be divided or propagated from leaf bases (pp.18–21). Over the years around one hundred cultivars in this group have been named. Unfortunately most are now lost or no longer recognized. Rare. **'Crispum Bolton's Nobile'**, 45cm (18in), was found on Warton Crag in North Lancashire around 1900 and grown by H. Bolton, although he may not have been the finder. It is the boldest form known. The fronds are often 10cm (4in) wide. The goffering is not as tight as in some forms but it is a beautiful fern. Rare. **'Crispum Moly'**, 45–60cm (18–24in), is a fertile form, probably more correctly classed in the Undulatum Group (see p.33). The frond tapers to a sharp point. Rare. **'Golden Queen'**, syn. 'Crispum Golden Queen', 30–38cm (12–15in), is a true crispum with deeply goffered fronds, irregularly variegated yellow. The variegation may cover a 7–10cm (3–4in) section of a frond or may be just a few stripes running from the midrib to the margin. It develops much more conspicuously in sun, but too much sun can burn the yellow areas, which turn brown by late season. For this reason it is best grown in semi-shade. In deep shade it remains green. This rare cultivar is grown to perfection at Stancombe Park near Wootton-under-Edge in Gloucestershire. Rare. **'Crispum Variegatum Bolton'** is virtually indistinguishable from 'Golden Queen'. Rare.

Asplenium scolopendrium
Fimbriatm Group

'Cristatum', 38cm (15in), has fronds crested at tip. Although the crest at the tip of the frond is wider than the lamina, the term 'Grandiceps', which usually describes this feature, is rarely used in *A. scolopendrium*. (Very heavily crested forms are named 'Capitatum' and 'Coronatum'.) Good forms of 'Cristatum' are uncommon in the wild. Usually the cresting at the tip is weak, being little more than branched ends, which often disappear under all but the most favourable conditions. Alternatively, the cresting develops with the maturity of the plant and the frond splits repeatedly lower down becoming 'Ramo-cristatum' (p.32). Common. **Fimbriatum Group**, 30cm (12in). Fronds slightly narrowed with margins finely but deeply serrate. Closely related to 'Marginatum' from which it differs by lacking a slim wing of tissue running the length of the fronds on the underside, either side of the midrib. This may have originated from 'Fissum-latum' or 'Fissile' both found by Mr Elworthy in the mid-nineteenth century. Common. **'Laceratum Kaye'** AGM, syn. 'Kaye's Lacerated', 20–30cm (8–12in). Fronds almost triangular, broadest towards base, margins deeply lacerated. Slightly variable from spores. This attractive cultivar was discovered in 1952 or 1953 growing on the stone walls at Kaye's nursery in Silverdale, North Lancashire. Jimmy Dyce always maintained he saw it first but I suspect Reg already knew it was there. Its name was not specifically published as 'Laceratum Kaye' until after 1959, so the one used here is arguably unacceptable under the International Code of Nomenclature for Cultivated Plants. The recommended name is 'Kaye's Lacerated', which I dislike. Quite rare.

'Marginatum', 38cm (15in), is perhaps the most common cultivar of *A. scolopendrium* occurring in the wild. A day's fern hunting in the Devon/Dorset borders will usually turn up a plant in this group. Typically the underside of the frond has a wing of tissue running more or less its entire length near the margin on its undersurface. The margin is also crenately lobed. Sometimes the wing of tissue is lacking but the name 'Marginatum' is still applied if the margin is lobed. The rarer form 'Supralineatum' has the wing of tissue on the upper surface. Sometimes, in 'Suprasoriferum', the sporangia creep around the frond margin onto the upper surface. Quite rare. **Muricatum Group**, 38–45cm (15–18in). The upper surface of the frond carries rows of pimples, in contrast to the glossy, reflective fronds of normal cultivars of the hart's tongue. Variable from spores. Many forms of this group have been raised over the years and we still have the gene pool to re-raise most, if not all again. Of greatest interest is 'Undulatum Muricatum', raised by Lowe in the later half of the nineteeth century. As the name suggests, the frond is undulating and muricate (rough-surfaced). I gathered spores of this cultivar from the grounds of Shirenewton Hall – Lowe's garden. At the British Pteridological Society Centenary Fern Show at Pebworth in 1991 a dwarf, tightly crisped form of 'Undulatum Muricatum', raised by long-standing society member Alf Hoare, won the Best in Show award out of about 250 plants. Quite common.

Asplenium scolopendrium
Ramosum Group

'Peraferens', 10–20cm (4–8in), is an extraordinary cultivar, with a horned frond tip enclosed in a small pocket or pouch. Rare. **Ramo-cristatum Group** (see also 'Cristatum'), 38cm (15in). Fronds branch repeatedly from near the base. All terminals crested. Strictly speaking more common than 'Cristatum'. Good forms are still being found every few years in the wild. I found one I call 'Feizor' in a limestone pavement in Yorkshire in 1972. Another find was in the vicinity of Lowe's home at Shirenewton. If the frond branches but the tip is not truly crested, the cultivar is 'Ramosum'. **Ramo-marginatum Group**, 30cm (12in). Fronds dark green, branch repeatedly from base to the tip of the frond, fan-shaped with narrow segments, the width of divisions varies from plant to plant. Strictly speaking marginate forms should have a wing of tissue running the length of the underside of the frond on either side of the midrib. In practice, it is often missing. Quite common. Included in this group are quite a large number of old forms not now recognized by name. However, careful study of existing material could easily result in the rediscovery of these and the selection of new distinct cultivars. The original form was raised by fern enthusiast Abraham Clapham of Scarborough around 1860. It reappears occasionally in modern spore sowings and is worth looking out for. Another of Clapham's selections, 'Keratoides', with an irregularly lacerated frond branching from near the base, also belongs in this group. 'Cervi-cornu' is similar except the branching is nearer the tip of the frond. The form 'Treble', raised by Fibrex Nurseries, was an unusual sparsely branched form with broader segments. It could now be extinct. **Ramosum Group** has fronds branching repeatedly. It can merge into 'Cristatum' where the branches become small and confined to the frond tip. Common.

Asplenium scolopendrium
'Sagittato-projectum Sclater'

↕ 7–20cm (3–8in)

🌿 Evergreen

Z 3

〰 Dry/Wet

🌐 Cosmopolitan, including
British Isles

Sagittato-cristatum Group, 20–30cm (8–12in). Fronds crested with arrowhead-shaped lobes at base. In the best examples of this group, the lobes at the base of the frond enlarge into a pair of lateral arms, which may be 10–12cm (4–5in) long and each terminate in a fan-shaped crest. The main part of the frond is broad and undulating and itself terminates in a broad crest. Rare. 'Alto', distributed by Fibrex Nurseries, was a dwarf form. **'Sagittato-projectum Sclater'**, 30cm (12in). An old cultivar which turned up recently in the Jim Lord collection (an offshoot of the Bolton collection). The fronds are arrow-shaped at the base; the rest of the frond is lacerated with a small flat crest at the top. Rare.

Undulatum Group, 30–38cm (12–15in). Frond margin deeply waved. Usually fertile. For simplicity I advocate that all undulate, thick-textured, fertile forms of *A. scolopendrium* are placed here and all undulate, thin-textured, sterile forms are treated as part of the Crispum Group. There are one or two fertile crispums eg. 'Crispum Moly'; I suggest they are better grouped here. 'Crispum Moly', being fertile, is an excellent source of new forms of true crispums. A selection from the Undulatum Group distributed from Holland is poor and hardly deserving of the name. I refer to these, rather unkindly, as wavy forms. Quite rare.

A. trichomanes AGM

Maidenhair spleenwort

A beautiful little fern with simple pinnate fronds. Pinnae usually spherical or short oblong. Rachis shiny dark brown or black. Common. There are many subspecies, all are extremely difficult to separate on vegetative characters but for the record the two commonest are subsp. *trichomanes* and subsp. *quadrivalens*. **subsp.** *trichomanes* is diploid and grows on acid or lime-free rocks and walls. Pinnae are almost round, usually smaller than subsp. *quadrivalens*. Rarer in the wild and rare in cultivation. **subsp.** *quadrivalens* is tetraploid and prefers calcareous rocks or mortared walls. Pinnae almost rectangular, often quite large. As far as I know all cultivars in cultivation are this subspecies. Occasionally the two subspecies hybridize producing an intermediate form, **nothosubspecies** *lusaticum*, which can be 30–38cm (12–15in) long. All forms need good drainage especially over winter in pots. All are fine in a shady border or more particularly in a rock garden.

'Incisum Moule', 12cm (5in), Dry, is like the type plant except the pinnae are prettily incised. Fertile and comes true from spores. Introduced by Moule, a fern nurseryman living in Ilfracombe, Devon in the nineteenth century. Recently, a crested form was raised by Stuart Williams. I have named it after him. 'Ramo-cristatum', 7–15cm (3–6in). Fronds branch with each terminal crested. ('Cristatum', where only the tip of the frond is crested, is uncommon.) Comes true from spores and persists in several localities in the wild where it was known in the nineteenth century.

Asplenium trichomanes
Ramo-cristatum

Athyrium

Northern hemisphere, temperate regions and tropics.

A large genus of deciduous ferns that have shortly linear sori with a slight bend at one end, often described as J-shaped. *Athyrium* is closely related to several other genera, eg. *Deparia*, *Diplazium*, *Lunathyrium* and *Cornopteris*, and some species seem to be moved around from genus to genus in horticulture. The best species for the garden is *A. filix-femina*. It is robust and grows well in damp shade. There are many species native to Eastern Asia that are hardy in Britain and deserve to be more widely grown. Unfortunately, they are difficult to name. However, once good books on Chinese, Himalayan and Japanese ferns appear in English, hopefully, it will be possible to get to grips with the problem. There seems to be an endless stream of lady ferns coming out of America, they appear to be either hybrids or cultivars of *A. niponicum* 'Pictum'. Several are described here, others not yet in general cultivation include 'Pewter Lace', and 'Soul Mate'.

✥ 50–75cm/20–30in

🍃 Deciduous˙

Z 6

〰 Wet/Dry

A. angustatum f. rubellum 'Lady in Red'

A beautiful selected clone of the species. The rachis and stipe a deep red. Much redder than the disappointing *A. filix-femina* 'Rotstiel'. Quite rare.

✥ 45cm/18in

🍃 Deciduous

Z 6

〰 Wet/Dry

A. 'Branford Beauty'

This is an erect, larger slightly more colourful form of *A. niponicum* 'Pictum'. I have not tried to grow the spores, although they would certainly appear to be viable. Reputed to be a hybrid with *A. filix-femina*. This fern is well worth growing if available. Quite rare.

✥ 30cm/12in

🍃 Deciduous

Z 6

〰 Wet/Dry

A. 'Branford Rambler'

A creeping form with *A. niponicum* 'Pictum' one probable parent. Less colourful, but creeping, eventually forming a patch. Quite rare.

A. filix-femina AGM

Lady fern

Fronds lance-shaped, very feathery, tripinnate. Dies down with first air frosts of autumn. Easily cultivated in cool, shaded, moist situations. Will grow in full sun if given plenty of moisture, eg. at pool margin. Usually more luxuriant on acid soils but still does well in alkaline sites. Propagate by division or spores, or rarely by bulbils (see Propagation pp.18–21). Common. Over 300 cultivars have been described over the past 150 years. Cultivars raised from spores frequently appear similar to the parent but are not the same. This can lead to the incorrect application of the parent name to the sporelings; it is, therefore, better to use the group naming system (see p.118). This tendency not to come true from spores sometimes leads to the raising of a completely new cultivar or the re-raising of a 'lost' treasure.

✥ 1–1.5m/3–5ft

🍃 Deciduous

Z 3

〰 Wet

🌐 Northern hemisphere, including British Isles

Capitatum Group, 60cm (24in). Tip of fronds crested but pinnae uncrested. 'Coronatum' is a selected form. Quite common. **'Caput Medusae'** Raised by Mapplebeck. Fronds branch repeatedly with twisted segments, resembling Medusa's hair. Rare: I have never seen a convincing specimen of this fern but the name, if not the plant, is in cultivation. **'Clarissima Bolton'** Found in Lancashire by Bolton and friend in 1893. Similar to 'Clarissima Jones' but smaller, slightly finer cut and somewhat inconstant. Like 'Clarissima Jones' this is aposporous but the offspring are usually depauperate. Rare. **'Clarissima Jones'** Found in North Devon by the fern nurseryman Moule in 1868, this is probably the most sought-after cultivar of any fern. Fronds tripinnate with all divisions slim and elongated producing a very elegant airy frond, perhaps 60cm (24in) across. It looks delicate but in practice is remarkably robust. It does not produce spores, so propagation is by division, but unfortunately the crowns are slow to split; it is therefore rare and plants have recently changed hands for £250 each. Apospory was first discovered on this variety. In the literature young plants raised are said to be indistinguishable from the parent, but folklore has it that they are depauperate. The few that I have raised have all been fine plants: the confusion may have arisen from the tendency of 'Clarissima Bolton' to produce depauperate offspring. **Corymbiferum Group** As Cristatum Group except the terminal crest is bunched in several planes, ie. not a flat fan. Crest narrower than the rest of the frond. Common. **'Congestum'** As the type plant except the rachis and pinnae midribs are reduced in length and the leafy parts of the frond overlap. 'Congestum Cristatum' is the crested form. Quite rare. **Cristatum Group**, 60cm (24in). Tip of fronds and pinnae crested; crest flat, ie. in one plane. Individual plants vary. Crest at tip of frond narrower than rest of frond. Common. See also Capitatum Group, Corymbiferum Group, Grandiceps Group and Percristatum Group for selected forms of the Cristatum Group. **Cruciatum Group**, 60cm (24in). Pinnae branch at their point of attachment to the rachis, opposite pairs of pinnae, therefore forming a string of crosses along the frond. Very unusual in the plant world and very attractive. Often referred to as 'Victoriae' in trade; in fact 'Victoriae' is the original member of this group and invariably a superior plant. 'Dre's Dagger' and 'Lady Victoria' are neat forms of Cruciatum, very similar to each other. Common.

Fancy Fronds Group, 15–20cm (6–8in), wet/dry. Raised by Judith Jones in her nursery Fancy Fronds in Seattle. These are dwarf lady ferns with fimbriate edges to the pinnae. Some are crested, some are plain. Rare. **'Fieldiae'**, 60–90cm (24–36in) is a form of Cruciatum Group. The true form is narrow-fronded, cruciate and more foliose than 'Victoriae'. Plants in general cultivation are spore-raised and, therefore, variable, but it is possible that the original clone still thrives in an out-of-the-way garden. First discovered in 1860, just pipping 'Victoriae' as the first cruciate lady fern found. Common. **'Frizelliae'** AGM (tatting fern), 15–22cm (6–9in), wet/ dry. Pinnate. Found by Mrs Frizell in Co Wicklow, Eire in 1857. Pinnae reduced to circular lobes along each side of the midrib, resembling tatting (handmade lace). Fronds dwarf (22cm/9in) and uncrested in the typical form, but most plants in cultivation are spore-raised and can grow longer fronds and crest at the tips ('Frizelliae Cristatum'), or branch at any point along the rachis ('Frizelliae Ramosum'). In lesser

Athyrium filix-femina 'Frizelliae'

forms some fronds may produce the occasional normal pinna. Because the pinnae are reduced to circular lobes 'Frizelliae' is less leafy than most lady ferns; it therefore loses less water in dry weather and can tolerate drier sites in the garden. Ideal in borders and rock gardens. Very pretty, very different. Common.

Grandiceps Group, 60cm (24in). As Cristatum Group except the crest at the tip of the frond is broader than the rest of the frond. Common. **'Minutissimum'**, 30–60cm (12–24in). A form I include with some reluctance. Plants under this name are imported from Holland. They are not necessarily minute and, in fact, tend to be rather variable in size, and they have no distinguishing feature apart from their supposed small size. Good plants do, however, form a clump around 30cm (12in) high which can be useful in garden design. Quite common. **Percristatum Group**, 60cm (24in). As Cristatum Group but tips of pinnules also crested. Quite rare.

Plumosum Group, 60–150cm (24–60in). A beautiful group of cultivars. Tri-, quadri- or even quinquepinnate. The frond divisions are more leafy than usual: they overlap and give a very feathery frond, hence "plumosum". Unlike plumosum forms of most other ferns, the plumose forms of lady fern are usually fertile. They do not come true from spores but, with patience, many fine things can be raised. Many forms have been named and a few are still in cultivation – all are worth growing but all are rare. Whether or not all the named forms in cultivation are correctly named is open to debate. **'Plumosum Axminster'** Discovered in a boggy meadow near Axminster in Devon by J. Trott in 1863. Tripinnate, almost quadripinnate, not the most feathery form of plumosum but well worth growing. It comes tolerably true from spores: it is not possible to tell the original clone from good sporelings. Rare. Improved sports occur from time to time in spore sowings, most notably 'Plumosum Elegans Parsons'. **'Setigerum'** A group of cultivars with all tips bristly. From spores crested ('Setigerum Cristatum'), simple ('Setigerum') or congested ('Setigerum Congestum') forms can be raised – all very pretty. Quite rare. Can hybridize with other cultivars, for example with 'Victoriae' it forms 'Setigerum Victoriae'.

Athyrium filix-femina
'Setigerum Cristatum'

'Vernoniae' AGM, 60cm (24in), is like the type plant except each pinnulet is briefly stiped, crispy and elliptical with a laciniated margin, particularly towards the tip of the frond. A beautiful, feathery form. Plants uncrested. Found by Mrs Vernon in the 1850s or 1860s. Common. 'Vernoniae Cristatum' is a crested form of 'Vernoniae' first raised from 'Vernoniae' by Mr Jones in 1873. 'Vernoniae Corymbiferum', which has a very heavy crest, might reappear in sowings. **'Victoriae'**, 90cm (3ft), was found near Drymen in central Scotland in 1861 by a student named Cosh. It is percruciate, that is the pinnae are cruciate (cross-shaped) on the rachis and the pinnules are cruciate on the pinna axis. The original

Athyrium filix femina 'Victoriae'
(original clone)

clone of this fern is very rare and changes hands at around £100 when available. It can be distinguished from other cruciate forms by its greater size when mature and its percruciate, airy frond form. It can only be propagated in true character by division. Unfortunately side crowns are produced infrequently, hence the rarity of the original clone. Good things can be raised from the spores but, as explained under Cruciatum Group (above), the spore-lings will almost certainly differ from the parent in detail. Over the years many sporelings of 'Victoriae' have been selected and given names. Any of these could well reappear in sowings. The most remarkable form is 'Setigerum Victoriae', a hybrid between 'Setigerum' and 'Victoriae', which has beautifully setigerate (bristly) pinnules coupled with the cruciate pinnae. Originally raised by Birkenhead at the turn of the century, lost, and then re-raised by Ray Coughlin in the 1980s, it is still in cultivation.

↕ 50–75cm/20–30in

🍃 Deciduous

Z 6

≈ Wet/Dry

A. 'Ghost'

Another presumed hybrid with *A. niponicum* 'Pictum' as a probable parent. Fronds erect and greyer than the parent. A very striking new introduction. The tallest grey fern in cultivation at the moment. Quite rare.

↕ 30–38cm/12–15in

🍃 Deciduous

Z 6

≈ Wet

A. niponicum 'Pictum'

AGM, syn. *A. goeringianum* 'Pictum', *A. iseanum* 'Pictum'
Japanese painted fern
One of the most popular garden ferns. Fronds mostly horizontal (spreading), bipinnate, lance-shaped, greyish-green with mauve midribs; the mauve colour suffuses into the lamina. Easy to grow if given sufficient moisture. For many years my plant struggled in a dryish spot under trees. I moved it to a rockery where its roots could run through the moist soil under the stones and it thrived. Common. There are several selected forms. The crested form is pretty with fronds and pinnae

Athyrium niponicum 'Pictum'

↕ 30–45cm/12–18in

🍃 Deciduous

Z 5

≈ Wet

🌐 Japan

crested. There are also forms selected for their especially good colour. Occasionally green forms are offered. These come up in spore sowings with the purplish form. They are a natural form and are worth growing in their own right. **'Silver Falls'**, 45cm (18in), wet/dry, has gracefully arching fronds, more silver than the parent, the silver colour can intensify as the season progresses. Quite common. **'Ursula's Red'**, 45cm (18in), wet/dry, has silver fronds flushing red from the centre. Quite common.

A. otophorum AGM

Eared lady fern
Fronds bipinnate, lance-shaped, fresh green with reddish stipe and veins. A very striking plant adding colour to a fern garden. For a lady fern it retains its fronds unexpectedly long into autumn. Common.

Athyrium otophorum

⬍ 45cm/18in

🍃 Deciduous

Z 5

〜 Wet/Dry

🌐 North America

A. pycnocarpon, syn. *Diplazium pycnocarpon*
Glade fern
Very distinctive fern with pinnate fronds. The pinnae are entire and well-spaced up the frond. Fertile fronds are produced later in the season; they are more erect and have slightly narrower pinnae. The rhizomes are short creeping, allowing a good colony to be formed in a few years. I grew this in a rather dry spot where it did tolerably well. I feel it could have been much taller in a moist site. Rare.

⬍ 30–45cm/12–18in

🍃 Deciduous

Z 6

〜 Wet

🌐 Japan

A. vidalii
Fronds bipinnate, new fronds reddish, more open and taller than *A. niponicum*. Another Japanese species with some colour other than green. Common.

⬍ 60cm/24in

🍃 Deciduous

Z 6

〜 Wet/Dry

A. 'Wildwood Twist'
Fronds grey with a little red near rachis. A hybrid with *A. niponicum* 'Pictum' as one parent. Not unlike *A.* 'Ghost', but smaller and twisted, unattractively in my view. Rare.

Blechnum Hard ferns, water ferns
Temperate and tropical regions.
Blechnum is a large genus of usually evergreen ferns, with the new foliage in spring often being pink. Some are well established as garden plants but many others deserve to be tried in temperate gardens. There are few native species in the temperate regions of the northern hemisphere, but there are many more in the tropics and southern temperate regions. All species prefer acidic soils, but most will do well as long as conditions are at least neutral (ie. pH 6.5 or less). Most species are dimorphic, that is sporing fronds differ from sterile fronds. Sporing fronds are usually more erect and longer with a narrower lamina. The sori are arranged along either side of the pinna vein, usually in a more or less continuous row. *Blechnum* are very similar to *Doodia*, except in *Doodia* the sori are arranged in 1 or 2 rows along either side of the midrib, and in *Blechnum* there is only one long continuous sorus along each side of the pinna segment.

⬍ 90–150cm/36–60in

🍃 Evergreen

Z 7

〜 Wet/Dry

🌐 South America

B. chilense AGM
Few popular garden plants can have been so frequently misnamed as this one. For many years it has been mistakenly known as *B. tabulare*, a small tree fern that grows in South Africa (at the summit of Table Mountain) and is not hardy. It is frequently confused with *B. magellanicum* (opposite), another South American species. More recently the correct name for this fern has been given as *B. cordatum*, but I believe this to be a similar,

Blechnum chilense

tropical species, and therefore wrong. For the moment, I will use *B. chilense*, especially as it has become quite widely accepted. Despite all its names, this is a magnificent garden plant with bold, dark green, pinnatifid fronds, up to 22cm (9in) wide. The rhizomes creep slowly, forming a large clump in a few years; outlying crowns can appear 12–15cm (5–6in) from established clumps. In time the oldest crowns produce short trunks up to 15cm (6in) tall. Given sufficient moisture it can achieve frond lengths of 150cm (60in), even in central England. Quite rare.

↕	38cm/15in
🌿	Wintergreen
Z	8
≈	Wet/Dry
🌐	New Zealand

B. discolor
Eventually a short-trunk forming species, even outdoors in Britain: the trunk can reach 15cm (6in) tall quite quickly. Fronds light green, pinnatifid, fairly narrow 5–7cm (2–3in) wide, erect in a shuttlecock. Side crowns are produced, forming a colony in time. Pinnae crowded on the rachis. The sporing fronds are very distinctive in the centre of the crown. Hardy with me for years in a dryish spot, but would do better in a moist site. Rare.

↕	45cm/18in
🌿	Evergreen
Z	6
≈	Wet/Dry
🌐	New Zealand

B. fluviatile
Ray water fern
Fronds 2.5–5cm (1–2in) wide, pale green, pinnate with short blunt segments. Sterile fronds spread out horizontally from the crown, surrounding erect sporing fronds. Brown scales along the rachis very noticeable. Hardy with me for years in a sheltered spot. Rare.

↕	90cm/36in
🌿	Evergreen
Z	8
≈	Wet/Dry
🌐	South America

B. magellanicum
This is truly one of the most exciting ferns that I have seen. As well as having narrow, pinnate fronds 90cm (3ft) or more in length, this fern produces a true and massive trunk. It is on record as having trunks 2m (6ft) tall. The best I have seen is slightly less than that but nevertheless a superb plant. The fronds are produced in large numbers in a regular crown from the erect rhizome (the trunk); there are no creeping rhizomes as in the commonly confused *B.chilense*. *B.magellanicum* has more than a passing similarity to a cycad. It occurs higher into the Andes than *B.chilense* so will hopefully prove to be at least as hardy, but for the moment I have put it in zone 8 as caution is wise with such a beautiful and rare plant. Rare.

↕	60–150cm/24–60in
🌿	Wintergreen
Z	7
≈	Wet/Dry
🌐	New Zealand

B. novae-zealandiae
A very handsome fern, common in New Zealand but only recently named. Fronds pinnate, 15–22cm (6–9in) wide, yellow-green, particularly when young. Pinnae broad, often overlapping. Seems hardy. Rare.

↕	60cm/24in
🌿	Evergreen
Z	9, possibly 8
≈	Wet/Dry
🌐	Australia

B. nudum
Fishbone water fern
Forms regular shuttlecocks of pinnatifid fronds. Pinnae long (5–7cm/2–3in) and tapering. Needs shade; can form large colonies in moist ground by streams but it is also good in a container. Larger plants can have slender trunks up to 60cm (24in) tall covered with black shiny leaf bases and are probably hardy in zone 8. Needs acid soil. Rare.

Blechnum penna-marina

↕	7–22cm/3–9in
🌿	Evergreen
Z	5
≈	Wet/Dry
🌐	New Zealand, Australia, South America

B. penna-marina AGM

Fronds pinnatifid, narrow (1cm/½in wide). Rhizomes creeping. Fertile fronds very erect and slightly longer than given sizes. Quite quickly forms a colony. Excellent as edging on peat block walls, as at Knightshayes in Devon. Can invade lawns and survive mowing! Nevertheless, it is not likely to be troublesomely invasive as the rhizomes are near the surface and easily removed where not wanted. Quite rare.

The species has been divided into several botanical subspecies. Two are commonly cultivated, both excellent garden plants with pinkish young fronds. There is a larger form, 15–22cm (6–9in) tall, probably **subsp. *penna-marina***, with smooth green pinnae, and a shorter form, 7–15cm (3–6in) tall, probably **subsp. *alpina***, with the pinnae more prominently veined and red-tinted. Both forms come from cold areas and have proved very hardy throughout Britain. **'Cristatum'** is a crested cultivar of the shorter reddish form.

↕	30–45cm/12–18in
🌿	Evergreen
Z	4
≈	Wet/Dry
🌐	Temperate northern hemisphere, including British Isles

B. spicant AGM

Sterile fronds spreading, narrowly lance-shaped, 2.5–5cm (1–2in) wide, pinnatifid, glossy dark green. Sporing fronds erect with narrower pinnae. A beautiful evergreen fern for all-year-round appeal. Neutral to acid soil only. Quite common. **'Rickard's Serrate'**, 30–45cm (12–18in). (Named by John Mickel, in 1994, not me!) I found this plant growing wild in North Wales in 1972 on a British Pteridological Society excursion. Since then it has been widely grown from spores. Like the type plant, except that it is bipinnatifid (pinnae are lobed), especially on the basiscopic side. Pinnae slightly sickle shaped. Similar forms were grown in the nineteenth century as 'Serratum' or 'Semilacerum'. Richard Rush raised 'Bipinnatifidum Rush' from my original find. It may still be in cultivation. The pinnae were more regularly, but more shallowly lobed along both sides than in 'Rickard's Serrate'. Rare.

Cheilanthes Lip ferns, cloak ferns

Distributed throughout the arid zones of warm temperate and tropical regions, including Mediterranean climate zones.

A large genus of ferns adapted to grow in rocky areas, often in deserts, where some humidity may linger. They are often covered with scales or hairs, particularly on the underside of the frond, to slow water loss by transpiration. In severe drought conditions many species roll up their fronds to minimize water loss. The common names refer to the sorus formed from the folded lip of the pinnae. *Pellaea* is another genus well represented in dry regions. The species listed has proven hardy in a cold greenhouse, well ventilated over winter, in

Cheilanthes tomentosa

central England; if it is to be grown outdoors it must have protection from winter wets. Critical botanists may not agree with the use of the term hair here, as opposed to scale. Most species are more or less evergreen; many of the fronds on a plant do shrivel over winter but only rarely do all perish.

C. tomentosa

Fronds grey-green, erect, narrowly lance-shaped, tri-pinnate-pinnatifid, with a few white hairs on the top surface and cream woolly hairs on undersurface. Fronds look slightly woolly. Pinnae triangular. A very pretty fern and the easiest cheilanthes to grow outdoors. Given good drainage and protection from winter wet (straw held in place with a slate), it has thrived with me in central England for over ten years. Rare. There is a form from the Santa Rita Mountains in cultivation. It is well worth growing, a neater plant with broader, leafier fronds.

⬍ 30–45cm/12–18in

▱ Evergreen

Z 6

≈ Dry

⊕ South-eastern USA

Cyathea

Widely distributed through montane forests of the tropics, with a few species occurring in cool temperate regions.

A large genus of about 600 species of tree ferns. All cyatheas can be distinguished from the rather similar genera *Dicksonia* and *Cibotium* by the presence of scales on the stipe. Fronds are generally lanceolate-triangular, with a long stipe. All species like a humid sheltered site with a lime-free compost and plenty of humus (for more cultivation details, see pp.14–17). All species listed will do well in a frost-free greenhouse. Each species should survive unprotected in the zone given; if wrapped up over winter it should also survive in the next coldest zone.

The species included here are only a selection: many more are available and many others have not been grown in temperate regions and may be worth trying whenever available. Sizes given are what might be attained in horticulture, specimens in the wild will often be bigger.

Cyathea australis

Cyathea australis trunk detail

↕ Trunk to 5.5m x 30cm/18 x 1ft
Fronds 1.2–3m/4–10ft

🌿 Deciduous (even in Australia)

Z 9, or perhaps 8

≈ Wet/Dry

🌐 Australia (Victoria, New South Wales, Tasmania)

↕ Trunk to 3m x 15cm/10ft x 6in
Fronds 1.2–2.5m/4–8ft

🌿 Evergreen

Z 10 possibly 9

≈ Wet/Dry

🌐 Norfolk Island

C. australis
Rough tree fern
Leaf bases and stipe covered with short, blunt spines, hence the common name. (Gloves are recommended for handling large specimens!) Exterior of top of trunk covered with the spiny frond bases, base of trunk covered with a mat of roots. Fronds bipinnate-pinnatifid, broad lance-shaped, glossy light green on upper surface but matt and slightly glaucous beneath. Long yellow-brown stipe is densely covered by dark brown scales when young, but these are shed as the frond matures, revealing a line of dark brown dashes along either side. Rare.

C. australis is fundamentally different from the two hardiest dicksonias, in its abundant covering of scales on the croziers and stipes and spiny leaf bases, which are arranged in symmetrical patterns throughout the length of the trunk. The frond, which tend to be a paler green, are also broader and more divided than those of the dicksonias and the frond stipes are long. Overall it is very distinct and comes closest to filling the need for a different type of tree fern for those already growing a dicksonia. In the wild it grows in the same areas as *Dicksonia antarctica* but at slightly higher altitudes and in more open sites. On balance it should, therefore, be at least as hardy as the dicksonia. However, it is relatively new to cultivation in Europe and its hardiness still needs to be proven over a few more winters. It needs a sheltered site with adequate water and good light; some direct sun is acceptable in early morning or evening. Plants offered in trade as *C. australis* are often *C. cooperi*.

C. brownii
Norfolk Island tree fern
Leaf bases covered with pale brown scales. Fronds bipinnate-pinnatifid, broad lance-shaped with orange-brown and white-brown scales. Spineless stipe has a line of white dashes running up either side. Superficially very similar to *C. cooperi*, cinnamon form, but differs in its more leathery laminae and by being very quick growing. Rare.

⬍ Trunk to 2.5m x 12cm/8ft x 5in
Fronds 1.2–2.5m/4–8ft

🍃 Evergreen

Z 9, possibly 8

〰 Wet/Dry

🌐 Eastern Australia

C. cooperi
Lacy tree fern

Fronds bipinnate-pinnatifid, broad lance-shaped. Stipe long, with pimples near base, generously covered in pale chaff-like scales and with a line of grey-brown dashes along either side. Stipe can become black in older plants, resembling *C. medullaris*. Trunk covered with scales near top, and 'coin-spotting', where there are leaf abscission scars, is sometimes visible lower down. Plants in circulation as *C. australis* or the South American *C. delgadii* may be this species. *C. cooperi* survived, but did not thrive, in a straw shelter outdoors for four winters in central England (zone 8). It would be better in a cool conservatory or outdoors in zone 9 or warmer. In nature it is absent from Victoria and Tasmania, yet is frost tolerant. Quite rare. **'Brentwood'** is a robust selection made in the United States. **Cinnamon form** is like the type plant but the rachis and stipe are covered with mats of cinnamon-coloured scales. **'Marleyi'** was introduced into cultivation in Australia. Differs from the type by being more graceful with all tips more finely pointed.

Cyathea cooperi

Cyathea cooperi trunk detail

C. cunninghamii
Gully tree fern, slender tree fern

This is the only species of tree fern common to both Australia and New Zealand. It appears very similar in both regions but the New Zealand plant appears to have a narrower trunk, particularly near ground level. Fronds bipinnate-pinnatifid, lance-shaped with no stipe. Bunches of small pinnae are produced at the base of each frond where it emerges from the crown, forming a 'wig'. Rachis is purple-brown, but black and spiny at the base and yellow brown towards the tip. It has mid-brown scales. Spines persist on old leaf bases encircling black trunk. In nature this fern is uncommon, usually growing in humid, dark gulleys. Coming from as far south as Tasmania it should be fairly hardy but its normally sheltered habitat would give it some frost protection. As a rule tree ferns with slender trunks are less hardy than fat-trunked species; however, experimentation with this in zone 8 with a very humid microclimate may prove rewarding, if it is not allowed to dry out. In my cold greenhouse this species is very quick growing, putting on about 15cm (6in) of trunk annually. In the wild in Australia it hybridizes with *C. australis* to make *C. x marcesens*. Spores are produced only on mature specimens when the trunk may be 6m (20ft) tall. They are, therefore, very difficult to collect, making this fern scarce in cultivation. Rare.

⬍ Trunk 6m x 7cm/20ft x 3in
Fronds 1–2m/3–6ft

🍃 Evergreen

Z 9

〰 Wet/Dry

🌐 New Zealand, south-east
Australia, Tasmania

⇕ Trunk 6m x 15cm/20ft x 6in
Fronds 1.2–2.5m/4–8ft

🍃 Evergreen

Z 9

≈ Wet/Dry

🌐 New Zealand

C. dealbata
Ponga, silver tree fern
Fronds bipinnate-pinnatifid, broad lance-shaped, dull light green on top, silver below, stipe silver. The silver powdery covering does not develop on very young plants. Stipe with brown scales and brown dashes along either side. One of the world's most beautiful ferns and the national emblem of New Zealand. Grows very happily in south-west Eire (zone 9 or 10) without protection. It regenerates but young plants are lost in severe winters much as happens with *Dicksonia antarctica*. In the wild this is a tree fern with a preference for slightly drier climates than most other species: therefore, plant in well-drained soil. Rare.

Cyathea dealbata

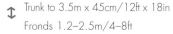

Cyathea dealbata leaf underside

C. dregei
Fronds bipinnate-pinnatifid, broad lance-shaped, deep green. Glossy brown scales on rachis. Grows at altitudes of up to 2100m (7000ft) in the Drakensburg Mountains, often in open sites by the sides of streams where it must endure severe weather. Large plants can survive grass fires as witnessed by their frequently grey trunks. Little is known about their cultivation in the northern hemisphere but this species is potentially one of the world's hardiest tree ferns. They should be given plenty of water, good drainage and plenty of light, ideally full sun in cold areas. Even in warm areas fronds die off annually. Plants have recently survived over winter in southwest Scotland and Gloucestershire. Rare.

⇕ Trunk to 3.5m x 45cm/12ft x 18in
Fronds 1.2–2.5m/4–8ft

🍃 Evergreen

Z 9, possibly 8

≈ Wet/Dry

🌐 South Africa

↕	Trunk to 4.5m x 10–22cm/15ft x 4–8in, Fronds to 3m (10ft)
🌿	Evergreen
Z	10, possibly 9
≈	Wet/Dry
🌐	New Zealand

C. medullaris
Black tree fern, Mamaku

Fronds bipinnate-pinnatifid to tripinnate, broad lance-shaped, very long, even in cold areas. Rachis and stipe black except on very young plants; lines of white dashes along either side of stipe. Base of stipe may be yellow if the dark brown scales are removed prematurely. Trunks are surprisingly heavy; plants imported as trunks from New Zealand are often rather slim, around 7–10cm (3–4in) in diameter, to mimimize weight and the costs of air freight. This fern has survived outdoors for a few winters at Portmeirion in

Cyathea medullaris

North Wales, Tresco in the Isles of Scilly and in south-west Eire (all zone 9), but the odd severe winter has usually been critical. More recently, I have seen it thriving on the Isle of Man. It grows about 30cm (12in) a year, sheltered from Irish Sea gales only by a *Griselinia* hedge. Fine in a greenhouse kept frost free. With care it makes a very quick-growing tree fern: in a cold greenhouse it may grow 7cm (3in) of trunk a year, although it is capable of much more – a plant I was shown in an Australian garden had grown almost 30cm (12in) a year. Avoid damp in crown in winter. Rare.

Cyathea smithii

↕	Trunk to 3m x 30cm/10ft x 12in Fronds 1.2–1.8m/4–6ft
🌿	Evergreen
Z	10, possibly 9
≈	Wet/Dry
🌐	New Zealand

C. smithii
Soft tree fern, Katote

Fronds bipinnate-pinnatifid, shiny above, narrowly lance-shaped with a short stipe. Mid-brown scales abundant on stipe, absent from laminae. Lines of small dark dashes along either side of stipe. This tree fern has the distinction of growing in the wild on the Auckland Islands, further from the equator than any other species of tree fern. It is also unusual in that its fronds are lance-shaped – very similar in shape and general appearance to *Dicksonia antarctica*, although the abundant scales will soon distinguish this from the dicksonia. Not common in cultivation, occasionally plants of *C. cooperi* are offered under this name. It may prove quite hardy but despite its provenance it is doubtful it will be as hardy as *Dicksonia antarctica*. Experimentation in zone 9 gardens will be interesting. Rare.

↕	Trunk to 1m x 7cm/3ft x 3in Fronds 1–1.5m/3–5ft
🌿	Evergreen
Z	10, possibly 9
≈	Wet/Dry
🌐	Papua New Guinea

C. tomentosissima

Fronds bipinnate-pinnatifid, dark green, lance-shaped. A mixture of orange-brown and pale brown scales abundant on stipe, rachis and even on pinnule midribs, making this a very beautiful fern. Trunk predominantly covered with pale brown scales. Ultimate pinnule segments are narrow and quite widely spaced giving the fronds an airy appearance. Only recently introduced into horticulture. Although it is found more or less on the equator in the wild, it grows at very high altitudes in alpine grassland where it experiences occasional short-lived frosts. Experimentation outdoors with larger specimens in zone 9 could therefore be successful. 'Highland Lace' seems to be no different from the type plant, but it is perhaps an attempt to introduce a pronounceable name. *Tomentose* means hairy (scaly) -*issima* means very, therefore the name is quite sensible. Rare.

Cyrtomium

Eastern Asia, especially Japan.

A small genus of evergreen ferns. Differences between species are subtle but in a garden all offer a dramatic contrast to other ferns and flowering plants. Fronds pinnate with a short stipe, pinnae entire, broad and pointed.

↕	45cm/18in
🍃	Evergreen
Z	7
〰	Dry/Wet
🌐	Japan, East Asia, Hawaii

↕	60cm/24in
🍃	Evergreen
Z	8, possibly 7
〰	Dry/Wet
🌐	Japan, East Asia

↕	60cm/24in
🍃	Evergreen
Z	6, undoubtedly also zone 7
〰	Dry/Wet
🌐	Japan, East Asia

↕	30cm/12in
🍃	Evergreen
Z	7
〰	Dry/Wet
🌐	Japan, East Asia

C. caryotideum

Fronds spreading, pinnate, pale green. Most pinnae have a prominent basal lobe (auricle). Usually fewer than ten pinnae along each side of frond. Rare.

C. falcatum AGM

Japanese holly fern

Fronds pinnate, very dark green and glossy. Usually more than ten pinnae along each side of frond. Some pinnae may have auricles. Reputed not to be reliably hardy but has thrived for many winters in central England. It may be advisable to protect the crown with a stone or straw over winter. Both the species and the cultivars are widely grown as houseplants. It has escaped and become established in the wild in Europe and North America. Common.

C. fortunei

Like *C. falcatum* except pinnae are pale, non-glossy green. Pinnae are also narrower and there are usually more than ten along each side of frond. Common. **var.** *clivicola* Japan, 38cm (15in), has lobed pinnae margins and more spreading fronds.

C. macrophyllum

Like other species but fronds more spreading, similar to *C. caryotideum* except it lacks basal lobe on pinnae. Usually fewer than ten pinnae on each side of frond. Very attractive. Rare.

Cyrtomium fortunei

Cystopteris Bladder ferns

Throughout cool-temperate regions.

A genus of around 20 species. The common name refers to the bladder-shaped indusium enclosing the sorus. Only one or two species are common in cultivation. They are beautiful in early spring, but are rather underused in the garden as, unfortunately, they die back rather early.

↕	38cm/15in
🍃	Deciduous
Z	3
〰	Dry/Wet
🌐	USA

C. bulbifera

Bulblet bladder fern

Fronds bipinnate-pinnatifid, narrow triangular, pale green. Plentifully furnished with bulbils along the rachis with a few on the pinnae midribs. These drop off and develop into new plants. Rare. A form in cultivation with incised pinnae was tentatively named 'Incisa' by Jimmy Dyce; a form with wavy pinnae has been discovered in the USA. Other North American species, such as *C. laurentiana* and *C. tennesseensis*, also produce bulbils but are rare in cultivation.

C. dickieana
Dickie's bladder fern

↕ 10–15cm/4–6in

✐ Deciduous

Z 4

≈ Dry/Wet with good drainage

⊕ Scotland

As *C. fragilis* (below) but smaller with pinnae set closer together on leaf axis, often overlapping. Pinnules also overlapping. This fern is only known from sea caves near Aberdeen in Scotland. Rare. On the basis of similar spore structure, a form that is widespread across Europe but is otherwise indistinguishable from *C. fragilis* has been grouped under this name. This may prove to be correct botanically but horticulturally the true *C. dickieana* is very distinct, constant in cultivation and comes true from spores. Ideal in rock gardens. Occasionally crested forms occur in sowings.

C. fragilis
Brittle bladder fern

↕ 15–20cm/6–8in

✐ Deciduous

Z 2

≈ Dry/Wet with good drainage

⊕ North America, Europe, including British Isles

Fronds usually bipinnate; pinnae and pinnules usually distant from each other. Pinnules compact, lance-shaped, pale green; pinnae triangular. A very welcome little fern in my garden as it is one of the first to put up new fronds in spring. Easy to grow in any soil but prefers some lime. Quite common. Apart from 'Cristata' there are no cultivars as such, but the appearance of the species varies throughout its range. The Victorian fern enthusiasts recognized several different species that have now all been sunk into this one. However, recently the Victorians have been proved right in other matters ferny, so I would not be surprised if modern biochemical research did not prove them right again here.

Davallia mariesii

Davallia

Mainly tropical with one hardy species from Japan.
A genus of very beautiful ferns with triangular, finely divided fronds produced on thick, scaly rhizomes that run along the surface of the growing medium. Unfortunately most species are frost tender.

↕ 22cm/9in

✐ Deciduous

Z 8

≈ Dry/Wet

⊕ Japan

D. mariesii AGM, syn. *Araiostegia pseudocystopteris*
Hardy hare's foot fern

Fronds finely divided, tripinnate, broad triangular with a long stipe. Creeping rhizomes covered with gingery scales. Hardy in a rock garden, if sheltered. Will eventually spread to become a small colony. Excellent for hanging baskets. Rhizome narrower than virtually all other davallias. Rare.

Dennstaedtia

Temperate regions, but absent from Europe.
A small genus of creeping ferns.

↕ 60cm/24in

✐ Deciduous

Z 9

≈ Dry/Wet

⊕ Australia

D. davallioides
Lacy ground fern

An attractive fern with tripinnate, triangular fronds on creeping rhizomes. Common in shady forests in Victoria, South Australia where it will take occasional light frost. Rare.

↕ 60–90cm/24–36in

🍃 Deciduous

Z 5

≈≈ Wet/Dry

🌐 North America

D. punctiloba

Hay-scented fern

Must have acid soil. Fronds bipinnate-pinnatifid, lance-shaped, hairy, yellow-green, erect carried on long creeping underground rhizomes. This fern can be invasive in moist, acid soil, perhaps a useful quality in large gardens. Can stand exposure to sun. In less than ideal conditions it normally stays where planted. Not the most beautiful garden fern as the fronds lack any real character and can collapse like a house of cards in dry conditions or severe winds. Glands on the fronds release the smell of new-mown hay when rubbed. The sori are similar to the dicksonia tree ferns, hence the synonym *Dicksonia punctiloba* in some old books. Quite rare.

↕ 15–30cm/6–12in

🍃 Deciduous

Z 9, possibly 8

≈≈ Dry/Wet

🌐 East Asia

D. wilfordii, syn.

Microlepia wilfordii

Delicate species with slender lance-shaped, bipinnate-pinnatifid, hairless fronds. Fertile fronds more delicately divided than sterile fronds. Rhizomes short creeping. Makes a most attractive tufted plant in a pot. I have grown this for over ten years in my unheated polytunnels with no problems. It should be hardy outdoors in zone 8; I have not tried. Rare.

Dennstaedtia wilfordii

Dicksonia

Upland regions of tropical and warmer temperate areas worldwide.

A genus of around 20 species of tree fern. Dicksonias differ fundamentally from cyatheas through the presence of hairs, as opposed to scales, on the frond stipe. Although all species are stated to be evergreen, in colder weather all may lose their fronds.

↕ Trunk to 6m x 75cm/20ft x 30in
Fronds 1.2–2.5m x 75cm/
4–9ft x 30in

🍃 Evergreen to −8°C (17.5°F)

Z 9 or possibly 8

≈≈ Wet/Dry

🌐 Australia, including Tasmania

D. antarctica AGM

Soft tree fern

Seemingly the hardiest of all tree ferns currently in cultivation, this has survived in my gardens in central England (zone 8), with protection, for 14 winters (min. recorded −15°C/5°F). Fronds bipinnate-pinnatifid, lance-shaped. Frond base covered with abundant purplish brown hairs. Stipe short or even absent. The trunk is made up of a central core of very hard woody vascular tissue. This is surrounded by old leaf bases through which root fibres grow. As the roots grow out they gradually increase the diameter of the trunk. In plants in cultivation the trunk is usually much shorter than the maximum figure given, and only up to 22cm (9in) in diameter. Inspection of the trunk of a plant growing in humid conditions in winter will often reveal actively growing pale-tipped roots; in summer active root growth is rarer. If possible grow out of winds

Dicksonia fibrosa

⬍ Trunk to 5.5m x 60cm/18ft x 24in, Fronds 1.2–2.5m x 75cm/4–8ft x 30in

🍃 Evergreen

Z 9 or possibly 8

〰 Wet/Dry

🌐 New Zealand

⬍ Trunk to 3m x to 30cm/10ft x to 12in, Fronds 1.8–2.5m x 60cm/6–8 x 2ft

🍃 Evergreen

Z 9 or possibly 8

〰 Wet/Dry

🌐 Brazil

⬍ Trunk to 3m x 7–10cm/10ft x 3–4in, Fronds 1–1.5m x 45cm/3–5ft x 18in

🍃 Evergreen

Z 10, possibly 9

〰 Wet/Dry

🌐 New Zealand

and in fairly humid environment (see also pp.14–17). It is a common misconception that *D. antarctica* comes from New Zealand. Common.

D. fibrosa AGM
Wheki ponga
This tree fern seems almost as hardy as *D. antarctica* here in central England – two well-protected plants have thrived with me over six winters outdoors and put on about 30cm (1ft) of trunk. Plants in cultivation are usually much smaller than the stated figure with trunks 22–30cm (9–12in) in diameter. Fronds bipinnate-pinnatifid, lance-shaped. They are darker green than *D. antarctica*, from which it differs most clearly in having up-turned margins to the pinnule segments, which make the upper surface of the frond feel rough when stroked gently (in *D. antarctica* the down-turned margins make the upper surface feel smooth). *D. fibrosa* also has a darker brown stipe and rachis with darker hairs than *D. antarctica*. The fronds of *D. fibrosa* tend to be shorter, too: a very useful indication of the greater suitability of this species for smaller conservatories. Much is often made of the way the old fronds hang down the side of the trunk to form a 'skirt', a characteristic shared with *D. antarctica*. The specific name, *fibrosa*, refers to the matted roots making up the very fibrous trunk. This species seems to make more roots on the trunk than *D. antarctica*. Quite common.

D. sellowiana
I have not grown this species outdoors but a plant with a 1.2m (4ft) trunk in a garden near here in Hereford (zone 8) has so far thrived for six winters without sustaining any checks to growth; in the view of the owner it is possibly doing better than *D. antarctica* and increasing its trunk height more noticeably. *D. sellowiana* is clearly very closely related to *D. antarctica* and *D. fibrosa*. In South America it does not grow any further south than southern Brazil

Dicksonia sellowiana

(about latitude 40), but it matches the other two species for hardiness, compelling evidence to support the theory that hardiness is not always the dominant character in determining natural distribution of a species. Although superficially very similar to *D. antarctica*, *D. sellowiana* has yellower hairs in the crown. As in *D. antarctica*, the margins of the pinnule segments are down-turned. The stipes of *D. sellowiana* are smooth, whereas in *D. antarctica* (and *D. fibrosa*) they are very slightly rough if rubbed. Rare. A fern in circulation in Australia as *D. sellowiana* lacks these distinguishing features; while clearly not typical *D. sellowiana*, its true identity remains a mystery but it is distinct in its own right from the other species.

D. squarrosa AGM
Wheki, rough tree fern
Less hardy than *D. fibrosa* or *D. antarctica*, this has struggled to do well in one of the warmest Cornish gardens (zone 9), but I have heard of several plants thriving in inner city gardens in Britain. Its trunk needs copious applications of water, which makes it difficult to establish outdoors. Fronds lance-shaped, bipinnate-pinnatifid with abundant dark brown hairs on the dark brown stipe and rachis. Rachis beneath

contrasting beautifully with the slightly glaucous green on the undersides of the pinnae. Stipes are set vertically out of the crown but the fronds arch out elegantly to form a spreading crown, reminiscent of vaulting in a church roof. The slender trunk is covered with a sheath of vertical dark brown or black leaf bases, which do not stick out from the trunk as they do in the other species. Some aerial roots are produced along the trunk but far fewer than in *D. antarctica*, *D. fibrosa* or *D. sellowiana*, hence the stipes remain conspicuous a metre or so below the crown. Unusually among the tree-like dicksonias in horticulture, this species produces side crowns up the trunk, as well as runners under ground to produce side shoots. If the main crown dies, do not throw away the stump: unlike in the other three species a new crown may appear. I have never grown this outdoors but it is ideal for a shady greenhouse where the trunk can be kept moist, or in a small conservatory where the shortish fronds reduce the pressure on space. Common.

Dryopteris

Worldwide, particularly common in temperate regions, but with some species in tropical zones.

This genus contains by far the largest number of good garden ferns. Most are hardy in zone 7 and should form a pivotal part of any fern border. Many species have scaly stipes which can be dramatically beautiful in spring as the croziers are unfurling. Some species are evergreen, some wintergreen, and some are completely deciduous. Many are extremely easy to cultivate and will even do well in poorly lit and poorly watered areas. Many species have been brought into cultivation over the last 30 years due to the worldwide collections of Christopher Fraser-Jenkins. Unfamiliar names given here are almost certainly his introductions. Many more of the 220 or so species, and even more numerous hybrids, could be included in this list, but I have restricted myself to those that I consider the most garden worthy. Other species are not in cultivation but may in time become more widely grown.

The descriptions here will not always enable a fern to be identified with certainty, but, hopefully, they will be adequate to determine what the plant is not. To really appreciate their distinctiveness, it is necessary to grow them.

⬍ 1–1.2m/3–4ft

▱ Wintergreen

Z 4

〰 Dry/Wet

🌐 Europe, including British Isles, Asia

D. affinis AGM, syn. *D. borreri*, *D. pseudomas*
Golden male fern
Fronds pinnate-pinnatifid, lance-shaped, dark green with golden-brown scaly stems. In winter they are likely to break and become untidy after gales or snow. Rhizomes erect with fronds forming a symmetrical crown. A magnificent garden fern that deserves to be grown more often, it is tolerant of several hours of sun daily, and is also more wind resistant than most ferns. The unfurling ginger-brown croziers in spring are stunning. *D. affinis* is very similar to *D. filix-mas*, but it can always be distinguished by the presence of a black zone at the base of the pinna where it is attached to the rachis. Even hybrids with some *D. affinis* in their blood show this mark. It can also be recognized by the almost squared-off tips to the pinna segments. Common. There are several subspecies which might be separate species, but it is generally agreed to leave them as subspecies. All subspecies are apogamous: this means that all cultivars come true from spores. Very rarely new sports arise; for

Dryopteris affinis subsp.
borreri

example 'Cristata Angustata' is a sport of 'Cristata'. **subsp. *affinis*** is very robust and very scaly. **subsp. *cambrensis*** has fewer scales but they are an attractive purplish-brown and the lamina is crisped. **subsp. *borreri*** has relatively few brown scales and looks most like *D. filix-mas*. But it is not always that easy – there are intermediates and hybrids. There are hybrids between each subspecies and *D. filix-mas*: they too are difficult to distinguish and are collectively called *D. x complexa*.

Cultivars of subsp. affinis

'Crispa Gracilis' AGM, 22cm (9in), evergreen, has very congested and crisped fronds, tips of pinnae upturned and seem pointed, dark green, not crested. Green and handsome throughout the winter in sheltered site. First grown by Dr Lyell, 1880s. Often grown as 'Crispa Congesta'. Common. **'Cristata'** AGM (king of the male ferns), 90cm (36in) or more, wintergreen, is a robust fern. The tips of the pinnae and the tip of the frond are crested, fronds mainly erect. Like 'Cristata Angustata' but fronds normal width and more erect. Common. **'Cristata Angustata'** AGM, 60–90cm (24–36in), wintergreen, is an elegant fern with narrow, long, arching fronds. Frond and pinnae tips crested. Quite rare. **'Pinderi'**, 60–90cm (24–36in), wintergreen, is uncrested with frond narrowed terminating in a slender point. Found in 1855 in the Lake District by the Rev. Pinder. A more compact form of *D. x complexa* 'Stableri'. Formerly considered a cultivar of *D. oreades*. **'Polydactyla Mapplebeck'** AGM, 1–1.2m (36–48in), wintergreen, is in some ways similar to 'Cristata' but the crests are much larger and not so neat. Strictly a grandiceps form as the crest is broader than the frond. Found in Westmorland in 1862 by Mapplebeck. Quite common.

Cultivar of subsp. cambrensis

'Crispa Barnes', 60cm (24in), deciduous, has fronds as in the type plant but with the lamina crisped. First recognized by J.M. Barnes in the Lake District in 1865 but since found in many places. It is, in fact, simply a well developed form of subsp. *cambrensis*. Common.

Cultivar of subsp. borreri

'Polydactyla Dadds', 90cm (36in), deciduous, is similar to 'Polydactyla Mapplebeck' but not so robust and the crests often little more than forks on the pinnae. This cultivar and Mapplebeck's form were recently differentiated by the notable botanist Christopher Fraser-Jenkins. Working in the herbarium at Kew he came across original named specimens of both forms and could instantly see that they were polydactylous (many-fingered crests) forms of different subspecies. It was then easy to name both forms in cultivation with confidence. Cultivars of *D. affinis* can reappear in the wild. I found this form on Keswick Railway Station in the Lake District around 1970 – clearly an escape from a nearby garden – nearly 100 years after it was first raised by Dadds in 1872. Quite common.

Cultivar of x complexa

'Stableri' (crisped), syn. 'Crispa Angustata', 60–75cm (24–30in), deciduous, is a dwarf form of 'Stableri' with slightly crisped pinnae. It does not appear to be in any of the early fern books and is probably a newish break, perhaps from the European continent. The synonym seems a more suitable name but is, unfortunately, apparently unacceptable. 'Stableri Heerlen' may prove to be correct. Common.

↕ 1–1.2m/36–48in

🌿 Deciduous

Z 5

〰 Dry/Wet or Wet/Dry

🌐 North-east USA

↕ 60cm/24in

🌿 Deciduous

Z 3

〰 Wet/Dry

🌐 British Isles, Europe

↕ 60–90cm/24–36in

🌿 Deciduous

Z 5

〰 Dry/Wet

🌐 North America

↕ 60–90cm/24–36in

🌿 Deciduous

Z 4

〰 Dry/Wet

🌐 North America

↕ 75cm/30in

🌿 Deciduous

Z 6

〰 Dry/Wet

🌐 Japan

↕ 60cm/24in

🌿 Deciduous

Z 3

〰 Wet/Dry

🌐 Europe, including
British Isles, North America

D. x australis (*D. celsa* x *D. ludoviciana*)

Fronds narrowly lance-shaped, erect, pinnate-pinnatifid. Pinnae bearing sporangia shorter than non-soriferous pinnae. As this is a hybrid the spores are rarely fertile but the rhizomes creep slowly, and frequently branch producing a mass of growing tips. Each of these can be removed to produce a new plant. Always rare, but so striking it is worth taking some trouble to find it. Much admired at the Chelsea Flower Show. Seems very unfussy regarding growing conditions but spreads well beside a pool here in Worcestershire. Rare.

D. carthusiana

Narrow buckler fern

Fronds bipinnate-pinnatifid, lance-shaped. Like *D. dilatata* (opposite) but fronds narrower and lance-shaped, with scales at frond base uniformly pale. Excellent for damp areas, quite at home in bogs. Quite common.

D. celsa

Fronds lance-shaped, pinnate-pinnatifid. In appearance not unlike a small *D. goldiana* – one of its ancestral parents. Quite rare.

D. clintoniana

Fronds pinnate-pinnatifid, narrowly lance-shaped on a long stipe. A broader form than *D. cristata* (below). A very elegant fern, easy to grow. If kept out of strong winds, it is ideal for most gardens. Quite common.

D. crassirhizoma, syn. *D. buschiana*

Fronds pinnate-pinnatifid, pale green and glossy, otherwise similar to *D. wallichiana*. Responds to a sheltered site. As with so many Japanese and east Asian species, the plants have 'colour'! The green is a yellow-green and quite eye-catching. Quite rare.

D. cristata

Crested buckler fern

Fronds pinnate-pinnatifid, erect and narrow. Very distinct among European species but closely related to several North American species including *D. clintoniana*. One of the rarest British ferns, only ever common in the Broads area of Norfolk, but easy to cultivate in a damp spot. Quite common.

↕	60cm/24in
🍃	Wintergreen
Z	5
≈	Dry/Wet
🌐	Japan

↕	60cm/24in
🍃	Deciduous
Z	6
≈	Dry/Wet
🌐	Japan

↕	1–1.2m/3–4ft
🍃	Wintergreen
Z	4
≈	Dry/Wet
🌐	Europe, including British Isles

Dryopteris erythrosora

↕	60cm/24in
🍃	Evergreen
Z	6
≈	Dry/Wet
🌐	Japan, China, Taiwan

D. cycadina AGM

Fronds pinnate; pinnae narrow, lance-shaped, dark green with serrated margins. Shape rather like *D. affinis* with all the pinna segments confluent (joined together). Fronds fairly erect and arching. Black scales on stipe. A very robust fern for colder gardens. It is one of the few ferns to regenerate naturally in my garden. Common. This fern is often distributed in error as *D. atrata*, which is a tender species. *D. hirtipes* is similar and may be hardy.

D. dickinsii

Fronds pinnate; pinnae linear with lobed margins. Beautiful yellow-green laminae contrast with dark scales on rachis. Similar to *D. cycadina* but more leafy and a paler green. Quite rare.

D. dilatata AGM

Broad buckler fern

Fronds tripinnate, triangular or broadly lance-shaped with pinnule margins often recurved. Distinguished from *D. carthusiana* by stipe scales having a dark central zone. One of the commonest British ferns. Common. There are a few good cultivars still in cultivation but several are possibly forms of closely related species.

'Crispa Whiteside' AGM, 60cm (2ft), is like the parent except the leafy part of the frond is crispy. First grown by Robert Whiteside and returned to general cultivation by Reginald Kaye about 25 years ago. Whiteside, a keen fern collector for over 50 years, considered this his best wild find. Common. **'Cristata'**, 60cm (2ft), deciduous, has small crests at tip of fronds and pinnae. A form with bunched crests can appear in sowings of 'Grandiceps', and a distinct form with more elegant, small, fingered crests recently occurred wild in the National Trust for Scotland garden at Inverewe in northern Scotland. Hopefully it still thrives there. This plant may be a cultivar of *D. expansa*. Quite rare. Another crested form, rare in cultivation, may in fact be a crested form of *D. azorica*. **'Grandiceps'**, 60cm (2ft), deciduous, has a large crest at the head of the fronds; pinnae also crested. Terminal head is rarely broader than the frond so strictly speaking plants rarely qualify as true grandiceps! Raised by Barnes. Quite rare. **'Lepidota'**, 45cm (18in), has the leafy parts of the laminae reduced in width, and the frond very scaly on the rachis and pinna midribs. Not crested. Rare. Sometimes called 'Hymenophylloides', which was a dwarf congested form, and 'Stansfieldii', which had thick and crispy pinnae. I believe both these latter cultivars are extinct. It could be that this and 'Lepidota Cristata' are cultivars of *D. expansa*. **'Lepidota Cristata'** AGM, 60cm (2ft), is a crested form of 'Lepidota' with the leafy parts of the laminae similarly reduced in width. A very elegant, airy plant. Common. **Recurved form** Origin unknown, possibly North America. Edges of pinnules are all curved down. Surprisingly attractive. Young plants reminiscent of *Gymnocarpium dryopteris*. Rare.

D. erythrosora AGM

Autumn fern

Glossy, bipinnate, triangular fronds emerge pink in spring, turning bronze then green as the season progresses. Stipe quite long. Sori on underside of fronds bright red, hence the species name: *erythro* (red) *sora* (sorus). One of the best garden ferns. The common name refers to the apparent autumn colours that the fronds produce in spring. There is possibly a complex of species in cultivation under this name (for example, *D. championii*, *D. cystolepidota*, *D. fuscipes*, *D. gymnosora*, *D. purpurella*). Not all have the red sori (eg. f. *viridisora*), but in every other respect seem to be the same fern. This fern is surprisingly evergreen; during snowdrop flowering (mid-February in Britain) the fronds are usually erect and unbroken and still have good yellow colour. Common. **var. *prolifica*** AGM, syn. *D. koidzumiana*, Japan. All leafy parts of the fronds are narrowed, giving a very airy appearance to the plant. Bulbils are sometimes produced.

D. filix-mas AGM
Male fern

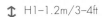

↕ H1–1.2m/3–4ft

🍃 Deciduous

Z 4

〰 Dry/Wet

🌐 Europe, including British Isles, Asia, North America

Fronds erect, pinnate-pinnatifid, mid-green, lance-shaped. Rhizomes usually erect but plants can develop a large number of crowns over the years. Along with bracken (*Pteridium aquilinum*) the commonest British fern, found almost everywhere in woods, on roadside banks, walls, waste ground, stream sides and so on. At higher altitudes it is replaced by *D. affinis* and *D. oreades*. The common name refers to the robust (masculine) nature of the fern – like almost all ferns it is hermaphrodite, producing both sex organs on the prothallus. The lady fern, *Athyrium filix-femina* is likewise hermaphrodite, being called lady fern because it is delicate (feminine). In the garden *D. filix-mas* is just about the most adaptable fern. All gardens have a dark, difficult corner, perhaps near the compost heap or site of the dustbin; *D. filix-mas* will thrive in such places with a little help during establishment. Furthermore, although easy to grow, it will not spread and take over a border, although sporelings may eventually grow where you do not want them. While common in Europe, it is very rare in North America being confined to calcareous woodland. It is possible the North American plant may turn out to be a different species – I have never grown it. Common; cultivars common, unless otherwise stated.

'Barnesii', 1–1.2m (36–48in), is potentially one of the tallest ferns for dryish borders. Fronds narrow, pinnate-bipinnatifid. Perhaps a parent of *D.* x *complexa* 'Stableri'. **'Crispa Cristata'**, 60cm (24in), has crispy fronds with lightly crested pinnae and frond tips. Pale green. **'Crispata'**, 60cm (24in), has fronds that are more leafy than usual with crispy pinnules. First found by Hodgson in 1864 in the Lake District. Quite common. **Cristata Group**, 60cm (24in), has pinnae tips lightly crested, frond tips more heavily crested, and fronds not crispy. Pale green. This name covers a number of different forms of cresting in *D. filix-mas*. **'Cristata Jackson'**, 60–90cm (24–36in), has pinnae with broad crests mainly in one plane. Prominent frond tip crest. **'Cristata Martindale'**, syn. 'Martindalei', 60–90cm (24–36in), was found in 1872. Crests small on all terminals but the characteristic feature is the way the pinnae in the upper part of the fronds are sickle-shaped (falcate), sweeping towards the tip of the frond. Quite rare.

'Decomposita', 60cm (24in), is like the type plant except fronds bipinnate-pinnatifid. Pinnae a little narrowed but similar texture to normal. A rather foliose cultivar. First discovered in Devon by Allchin. Quite common. **'Depauperata Padley'**, 45–60cm (18–24in), is misleadingly named as the fronds are not really depauperate. Bipinnate fronds with confluent pinnules. A pretty fern, well worth growing when available. Found by Padley in 1868 on Exmoor. Quite rare. **'Grandiceps Wills'** AGM, 60–90cm (24–36in), was found by John Wills in Dorset in 1870. Frond tip has a broad multi-branched crest. Small pinnae crests. Very robust once established.

Dryopteris filix-mas
'Depauperata Padley'

There are fine stands at Harlow Carr Gardens in Harrogate. Plants in cultivation are no doubt all sporelings but seem identical to the original. Jimmy Dyce found an identical form wild on Whitbarrow in the Lake District in the 1980s. Quite rare.

'**Linearis**', 60cm (24in), is an old cultivar, named by Wollaston in the nineteenth century but with an unknown origin. Fronds darker green, bipinnate with very narrow, leathery pinnules. Tends to be slightly depauperate, sometimes leading to misidentification as 'Depauperatum'. The plant looks very delicate and almost wispy, but in reality it is very tough, being able to tolerate windy spots in the garden. '**Linearis Congesta**', 15–30cm (6–12in), is a congested, dwarf form of 'Linearis'. Rare. '**Linearis Polydactyla**', syn. 'Linearis Cristata', 75cm (30in), is a crested form of 'Linearis'. Fronds bipinnate; pinnules narrowed and leathery; fronds and pinnae crested. Crests often long and fingered, hence 'Polydactlya' is often a more appropriate name. Darker green than most *D. filix-mas* cultivars. The crested forms are much commoner than straight 'Linearis'. In the 1980s Philip Coke raised one with a very wide pendulous head. The name '**Polydactyla**' occasionally appears in lists. I cannot remember ever seeing the plant. 'Linearis Polydactyla' or 'Polydactyla Dadds' in *D. affinis* may be the fern intended.

D. goldiana
Goldie's fern
Fronds pinnate-pinnatifid, broad lance-shaped, but not triangular, with a long stipe. Very leafy, slightly arching, golden-green; not, however, named for its colour but for its discoverer. Rhizomes short creeping, gradually forming a clump. One of the tallest ferns for a sheltered shady garden. *D. monticola* is similar and native to eastern Asia. Quite common.

D. intermedia
Very lacy, tripinnate species. Fronds lance-shaped, almost oval, pale green, covered with minute glands, particularly on the underside. Overall rather similar to European *D. carthusiana*, but distinct. Rare.

D. lacera
Fronds pinnate-pinnatifid, narrowly triangular. Spores are produced at the tip of the frond on just a few pinnae which are smaller than would be expected. In addition these pinnae shrivel up once the spores are shed, the remainder of the frond staying green into autumn. Prefers acid soil, but not essential. Rare.

D. lepidopoda
Fronds lance-shaped or narrowly triangular, pinnate-pinnatifid. This fern was originally collected as *D. wallichiana*: when it produced pink fronds it was recognized as a new species. It is superficially similar to *D. wallichiana* except for the pink new fronds, which go bronze then green within a few weeks of unfurling. Also the lamina is a little glossy on the upper surface. Rare.

Dryopteris lepidopoda

↕ 1–1.2m/36–48in

✤ Deciduous

Z 4

≋ Wet/Dry

⊕ North America

↕ 60cm/24in

✤ Wintergreen

Z 4

≋ Dry/Wet

⊕ North America

↕ 45–60cm/18–24in

✤ Deciduous

Z 7

≋ Dry/Wet

⊕ Eastern Asia

↕ 60cm/24in

✤ Deciduous

Z 7

≋ Dry/Wet

⊕ Himalaya

↕ 60–75cm/24–30in

🍃 Wintergreen

Z 4

≈≈ Wet/Dry

🌐 North America

↕ 60–90cm/24–36in

🍃 Wintergreen

Z 7

≈≈ Dry/Wet

🌐 Himalaya

D. marginalis

Fronds triangular, bipinnate, bluish-green. Rhizomes erect and slow to branch, hence plants can produce a magnificent single crown. Name refers to the presence of the sori along the margins of the pinnulets. Very common in North America where it seems to fill the role that *D. filix-mas* plays in Europe. Good robust garden fern. Quite common.

D. neorosthornii

Fronds lance-shaped, bipinnate. Pinnules slightly squared at tip and crenately lobed along the sides. Scales on rachis are larger, more numerous and blacker than *D. wallichiana*. Stipe short, very scaly. This must be the most striking of this group of dryopteris. In spring the uncurling croziers are black and wonderfully mysterious. Rare.

Dryopteris neorosthornii (left), *Dryopteris lepidopoda* (right)

↕ 45–90cm/18–36in

🍃 Deciduous

Z 4

≈≈ Dry/Wet

🌐 Europe, including British Isles, Asia

D. oreades, syn. *D. abbreviata*
Dwarf male fern
Fronds lance-shaped, pinnate-pinnatifid. Pinnules frequently crisped up. Unless this species is in typical form it is easily confused with *D. x complexa* and *D. filix-mas*: both ferns contain genetic material of *D. oreades*. It is distinguished from *D. filix-mas* by the rounded, crenate teeth on its pinnae segments, and from *D. affinis* subsp. *cambrensis* by its lack of a dark spot at the point where the pinna midrib joins the rachis. The Asian form, which comes from Turkey, is slightly different. The common name is confusing as, in low-level woods in mountainous districts, this fern can easily have fronds 90cm (36in) long. One of the first ferns to die down in winter, but its crispy fronds make it a pretty garden plant. Quite common.

↕ 45–60cm/18–24in

🌿 Evergreen

Z 8

≈ Dry/Wet

🌐 East Asia

↕ 60cm/24in

🌿 Deciduous

Z 7

≈ Dry/Wet

🌐 North-east Asia

↕ 60–90cm/24–36in

🌿 Deciduous

Z 6

≈ Dry/Wet

🌐 Mexico

↕ 60cm/24in

🌿 Evergreen

Z 8

≈ Dry/Wet

🌐 Japan

↕ 45–60cm/18–24in

🌿 Deciduous

Z 6

〰 Dry/Wet

🌐 Japan

↕ 60cm/24in

🌿 Deciduous

Z 7

≈ Dry/Wet

🌐 Western Himalaya

D. pacifica

Young fronds reddish, tips pointed, curving slightly towards the tip of the frond. Like *D. erythrosora* but more elegant. Quite rare.

D. polylepis

Lamina lance-shaped, pinnate-pinnatifid. Pinnae lobes squared at tip as in *D. affinis* but segments slightly narrower and longer. Quite rare.

D. pseudofilix-mas

Fronds lance-shaped, pinnate-pinnatifid. Very similar to *D. filix-mas* but mentioned here as further evidence of hardy ferns occurring at high altitudes in the tropics. Quite rare.

Dryopteris sieboldii

D. pycnopteroides

Fronds dark green, pinnate with regularly serrated margins. Pinnae almost overlapping. Quite rare.

D. sieboldii

Fronds leathery, triangular or broadly lance-shaped, pinnate, occasionally bipinnate at base, pale green. Pinnae margins finely serrate but at a glance appear smooth, quite unlike any other dryopteris. Common.

D. stewartii

Fronds broadly triangular, bipinnate-pinnatifid to tripinnate, pale green. Quite rare.

↕	60cm/24in
⌀	Wintergreen
z	5
≋	Dry/Wet
⊕	India, Nepal

D. sublacera

Fronds broadly lance-shaped, bipinnate, but pinnules lobed at base; dark dull green above, pale silvery green below. Pinnae taper to tip. Rachis and stipe covered with dark brown scales. A robust plant worth growing when available. Quite rare.

↕	60–90cm/24–36in
⌀	Deciduous
z	7
≋	Dry/Wet
⊕	Japan

D. tokyoensis

Fronds erect, narrowly lance-shaped, pinnate, pale green. Pinnae are wide at their base gradully tapering to a point. A very distinctive fern, deserving to be grown more widely. I have seen it in an Italian garden approaching 1.2m (4ft) tall. Quite common.

↕	30–60cm/12–24in
⌀	Wintergreen
z	6
≋	Dry/Wet
⊕	Eastern Asia

D. uniformis

Fronds broadly lance-shaped, bipinnate, leathery. Black scales a feature on croziers. Quite rare. 'Cristata' is a crested form in some collections. Also quite rare.

↕	60–120cm/24–48in
⌀	Wintergreen
z	6
≋	Dry/Wet
⊕	Hawaii, Mexico, Jamaica, Himalaya

D. wallichiana AGM, syn. *D. parallelogramma*

Fronds lance-shaped, pinnate-pinnatifid. Pinnae segments neatly squared off at the tips. Stipe short. Stipe and rachis liberally covered with (usually) brown scales; the form most common in cultivation, however, has black scales. Common. It was refound in the wild near Darjeeling by Fraser-Jenkins, who has segregated it as subsp. *himalaica*. subsp. *nepalensis*, also described by Fraser-Jenkins, is a robust form with an attractive glossy upper surface. It is intermediate between *D. wallichiana* and *D. lepidopoda*. Plants from all parts of the natural range appear to be hardy in Britain. Rare.

Gymnocarpium

Northern temperate zones.

A small genus of charming little ferns. The thin, papery lamina is almost always held at close to 90 degrees to the stipe. All species can be propagated by division or from spores. Albeit rarely, many of the species cross in nature. The resulting hybrids can usually be detected by abortive spores; no hybrids have been found in the British Isles. The whole genus is ideal for cultivation in a shady herbaceous border or among rocks.

↕	22–30cm/9–12in
⌀	Deciduous
z	3
≋	Wet/Dry
⊕	Europe, including British Isles, Asia, North America

G. dryopteris AGM

Oak fern

Fronds pale green (blue-green in deep shade), tripinnate, triangular. Stipe erect, delicate, long, with few colourless scales but no hairs. Rhizomes far creeping. A delightful little fern but can become invasive in neutral to acid, well-watered soils. Common. 'Plumosum' AGM (plumose oak fern) is broader, more luxuriant and foliose, with broader laminae; pinnules and pinnae overlapping. Another beautiful fern, first discovered in the early 1900s by Mr Christopherson on a limestone hill in the Lake District. The lime may have been leached out of the site as this is usually an acid-loving fern. Possibly more correctly called 'Foliosum' as it is fertile, coming true from spores. Common.

↕	15–30cm/6–12in
✿	Wintergreen
Z	7
≈	Wet/Dry
⊕	East Asia

G. oyamense

Fronds a beautiful blue-green, pinnate-pinnatifid. Lamina triangular, but less markedly so than other species in the genus. A beautiful fern. It is surprisingly hardy: I have grown it outdoors for years with little effort, and it also seems quite hardy in my unheated polytunnels. It is often evergreen, unlike other ferns in the genus, and it would not surprise me greatly if eventually a new genus is created to accommodate it. Rare.

Gymnocarpium oyamense

↕	15–30cm/6–12in
✿	Deciduous
Z	3
≈	Dry/Wet
⊕	Europe, including British Isles, Asia, North America

G. robertianum
Limestone polypody

Fronds pale yellowish-green, bipinnate-pinnatifid, triangular with a long stipe covered with minute stalked glands. Not so leafy as *G. dryopteris* with the margins of the lamina often down-turned. The lamina is not so strongly angled from the stipe as in other species. Limestone polypody likes to grow on limestone screes and rockwork. In Britain it is uncommon in native habitats but occurs from time to time on old walls. Rare.

Histiopteris

Distributed throughout the tropics and temperate regions.
A very small genus closely related to *Pteridium* (bracken).

↕	60–120cm/24–48in
✿	Deciduous
Z	7
≈	Wet/Dry
⊕	Tropics and temperate southern hemisphere

H. incisa
Water fern, bat wing fern

Frond tripinnate, triangular, pale glaucous green. Basal pinnules adjacent to, and tending to clasp, the main rachis (hence bat wing fern). Rhizomes far creeping. Invasive when established, not unattractive but can become weedy. Occasionally imported on trunks of *Dicksonia antarctica* from Australia. Needs acid soil and good protection over winter. Quite rare.

Hypolepis

Warm temperate or tropical areas.
A genus of ferns related to *Pteridium* (bracken). Like bracken, they spread, but not normally so rapidly. Various species are occasionally introduced on trunks of *Dicksonia antarctica* from Australia. Unless protected from all but the slightest frost, they do not persist.

↕	30–38cm/12–15in
✿	Deciduous
Z	7
≈	Dry/Wet
⊕	New Zealand

H. millefolium
Thousand-leaved fern

Fronds broadly ovate, tripinnate-pinnatifid. Stipe covered with brown hairs. Creeping rhizomes. Not usually invasive, this fern can spread to form a very attractive, good-sized clump. The finely divided leaves and the clumping growth habit instantly separate it from almost every other garden fern. Unfortunately this has not done well with me in my alkaline gardens; however, a friend only 20 miles away grows it beautifully on her slightly sandy, acidic soil. Rare.

Lophosoria

Central and South America.
A genus of a single species closely related to *Cyathea*, resembling a small tree fern.

Hypolepis millefolium

⬍ Trunk to 1m/3ft
　 Fronds to 2m/6ft

🌿 Evergreen

Z 9, possibly 8

〰 Wet/Dry

🌐 Central and South America

L. quadripinnata

Frond triangular, tripinnate-pinnatifid, fairly leathery. Usually glaucous beneath. Plants from southern Chile, in the far south of its natural range, are probably more hardy but rarely seem able to produce a trunk. Trunk or rhizomes covered with golden hairs. It is very variable; in time the southern type may be recognized as a separate species. I have grown the Mexican plant outdoors in my tree fern shelter for four or five years. It has survived but does not thrive and has still not started to produce a trunk. I have heard of *L. quadripinnata* of more southerly origin doing well in south-west Britain, producing large fronds but, again, no trunk. This is a beautiful, potentially dramatic fern that deserves to be more widely grown. Rare.

Lygodium

Mainly tropical with one or two temperate species.
Lygodiums are climbing ferns. Their roots are in the ground but their fronds are of virtually indeterminate length as they climb up through vegetation. The pinnae midribs and the rachis have the ability to wind round any support, just like a pea tendril. Sporing pinnules smaller and neater than others. Spores are green and must be sown soon after harvest.

⬍ 1–1.5m/3–5ft, much taller in
　 the wild

🌿 Deciduous

Z 9

〰 Dry/Wet

🌐 South-east Asia, Japan

L. japonicum

Frond tripinnate and narrowly triangular but, because of this fern's climbing habit, the shape is rarely obvious. Pinnae triangular, spreading horizontally. A beautiful and fascinating plant well worth taking the trouble to grow. I know of one garden in England where it has survived, so far, at the base of a warmish wall. The soil is a well-drained loam with some organic fibre added, and the fern gets some shade in summer. I have not tried it outdoors yet. It is wise to mulch the crown to protect against cold winters. Very easy to grow from spores: it was the first fern I ever propagated back in 1965 and I had thousands of plants that I did not know what to do with. Quite common.

Matteuccia

Northern temperate zones.
Although a small genus, this is a very important one in temperate gardens where some moisture is available.

↕ Fronds: Vegetative 60–90cm/ 2–3ft, Fertile 15–22cm/6–9in

🍃 Deciduous

Z 7

≋ Wet/Dry

🌐 Asia

M. orientalis

Fronds lance-shaped, pinnate-pinnatifid, spreading. Stipe quite long with pinnae not markedly reduced in length at base of frond. Fertile fronds spreading, or even drooping, initially green but soon turning brown, lacking any lamina. Produced on a creeping caudex (rhizome). A pretty fern for a sheltered spot, its spreading foliage makes it distinctive in the garden. Deserves to be grown more widely. Quite common.

↕ Fronds: Vegetative 60–120cm/ 3–4ft, Fertile 30cm/12in

🍃 Deciduous

Z 3

≋ Wet

🌐 North America

M. pensylvanica

Ostrich fern, shuttlecock fern

I will be criticized by botanists for recognizing this fern as being different from *M. struthiopteris* at specific level. It is, however, fairly distinct, with both species deserving to be grown. It differs from *M. struthiopteris* in that the base of the stipe is glaucous and the fronds are less erect, giving a more open shuttlecock. Rare.

↕ Fronds: Vegetative 1–1.5m/ 3–5ft, Fertile 30–45cm/12–18in

🍃 Deciduous

Z 3

≋ Wet

🌐 Central Europe

M. struthiopteris AGM, syn. *M. germanica*

Ostrich fern, shuttlecock fern

Fronds lance-shaped with pinnae, markedly reduced in length, right to the base, pale yellow green, pinnate-pinnatifid, mainly produced in a single flush in spring as a beautiful, almost erect, shuttlecock. Stipe almost absent. Fertile fronds are produced in autumn and are completely given over to spore production. They lack laminae and are very dark green when first produced but soon turn brown. Do not mistake them for evidence of disease. The spores are green and ripen in midwinter. They are not viable for long and need to be sown immediately after collection. I cut a sporing frond around Christmas. I leave it to dry on a piece of white paper for about half an hour, then, as if by a miracle, thousands of spores are released onto the paper. The main caudex (rhizome) is erect and, eventually, in suitable damp conditions a small trunk up to 15cm (6in) tall can develop. Creeping stolons 4–15mm (about ⅛–½in) in diameter also grow. These do not produce occasional fronds along their length but rather, when ready, suddenly develop a new crown. In time quite a colony can be formed. If the new crowns appear in the wrong place they are easily removed and replanted elsewhere. The stolon is near the surface so, despite its creeping nature, can be kept in check with little difficulty. Plant in shade otherwise sun may burn fronds by midsummer. Common.

Microsorum

Tropical and warm temperate areas.
A group of ferns closely related to *Polypodium*.

⬍ 30cm/12in

🍃 Evergreen

Z 9

〰 Dry

🌐 Australia, New Zealand

M. diversifolium

Kangaroo fern

Frond pinnatifid, occasionally simple, glossy, leathery produced on creeping rhizomes. Occasionally introduced on the trunks of *Dicksonia antarctica* where it can persist with little attention. Can be grown on a free-draining bank, as at Par in Cornwall, or more usually as an epiphyte on trees, as at Dereen and other gardens in south-west Eire. I have seen it festooning trees from ground level to 5–6m (15–20ft) above the ground in several Irish gardens. Although I have not attempted to grow it outdoors in central England, it has done well in an unheated polytunnel. A closely related Australasian species, *M. scandens*, is slightly more delicately cut, but also slightly less hardy. Rare.

Microsorum diversifolium smothering a tree trunk

Onoclea

North America.
A genus containing a single species, but one of the best and most distinctive ferns for general cultivation.

⬍ 60cm/24in

🍃 Deciduous

Z 2

〰 Wet

🌐 North America

O. sensibilis

Sensitive fern

Fronds triangular pinnate, blue-green with crenately lobed pinnae. Stipe long. Creeping rhizomes, therefore spreads rapidly in wet ground. Fertile fronds, produced late summer, have laminae replaced by spore-carrying beads. As with *Matteuccia* the spores are green, ripen in midwinter and can be induced to shed in a heated room in around half an hour. Spores need to be sown as soon as possible after shedding. Common.

O. sensibilis is ideal for planting in a damp site where there is plenty of room; in small gardens it may become a little invasive, but its distinct foliage usually makes it a welcome invader. The rhizomes are near the soil surface and can usually be peeled back from areas where the fern is not welcome. A form in cultivation has red fronds in spring. It is rare but worth hunting down – the red colour persists in the stipes almost all season but the laminae eventually turn green. It is called sensitive fern because it dies down with the first autumn frost; conversely, late spring frosts do not seem to be damaging. I have recently been given a dwarf form which may prove constant.

Onychium

Western Asia.

A small genus of several closely related species. The following has proved tolerably hardy with me in north Herefordshire in sheltered niches in the garden and I have seen it flourishing in a cold Staffordshire garden.

O. japonicum

Carrot fern

Fronds triangular tri- or quadripinnate at base. Stipe long, dark yellow at base. A very pretty fern looking like a carrot leaf. Rare.

⬍ 30–45cm/12–18in

🍃 Deciduous

Z 8, possibly 7

〰 Dry/Wet

🌐 East Asia

Osmunda

Mainly temperate regions, worldwide.

A genus of about 10 species of majestic plants well suited to water gardens or damp places. They are the largest garden ferns hardy in areas that are too cold for tree ferns. Sporangia are produced on pinnae of reduced size that usually lack any lamina. Early in the season, when the spores are unripe, the sporangia are green; they soon turn black or brown as the spores ripen. The spores are shed by midsummer leaving the sporangia brown and shaggy for most of the growing season. The spores are green and need to be sown within a month of collection. Osmundas generally prefer acidic soil conditions, but do well in alkaline gardens, if given a good fibrous compost. With adequate moisture, osmundas will grow satisfactorily in full sun.

O. cinnamomea AGM

Cinnamon fern

Fronds of two types. Vegetative fronds green, lance-shaped, pinnate-pinnatifid, produced in a shuttlecock. Fertile fronds are slightly taller than vegetative fronds and lack any green lamina. The pinnae are covered with cinnamon-coloured sporangia and confined to the top half of the frond. These pinnae are held almost upright close to the rachis, giving the frond the shape of a slender pampas grass flower stem. Several sporing fronds are produced in the centre of the ring of vegetative fronds, creating a stunning effect. There are brown hairs mixed within the sporangial clusters. The sporing fronds wither in about three weeks, once the green spores are shed, but the vegetative fronds persist until autumn. This is one of my favourite ferns. Quite rare.

⬍ 60–120cm/24–48in

🍃 Deciduous

Z 2

〰 Wet

🌐 North America

O. claytoniana AGM

Interrupted fern

Fronds lance-shaped, pinnate-pinnatifid. Sterile fronds green throughout, forming a slightly open shuttlecock. Fertile fronds differ in being erect and having two or three sets of sporing pinnae mid-frond. In these pinnae the green lamina is completely replaced by massed sporangia. The sporangia blacken as they ripen and shrivel soon after shedding the green spores. The frond is thus interrupted, hence the common name. A fascinating garden fern that is easy to establish in a damp spot. Quite rare.

⬍ 60–90cm/24–36in

🍃 Deciduous

Z 2

〰 Wet

🌐 North America

↕ 60–120cm/24–48in

🌿 Deciduous

Z 7

≈≈ Wet

🌐 Origin unknown

O. gracilis, syn. *O. regalis* var. *gracilis*
Very similar to *O. regalis* 'Purpurascens' except smaller, much more delicate and fronds are red in spring. The red fronds with green sporangia on the terminal pinna are a beautiful sight. The differences between this fern, *O. regalis* 'Purpurascens' and *O. regalis* var. *spectabilis* need further investigation. Rare.

O. regalis AGM
Royal fern, flowering fern
Fronds broadly lance-shaped, bipinnate; pinnules oblong-ovate with smooth margins. Stipe long and smooth. Rhizomes branched, erect, massive, over many decades eventually becoming 30–60cm (1–2ft) tall and the same, or more, across. Fertile fronds produced among the first flush of fronds in spring are erect. Later, vegetative fronds are often more spreading and usually longer. Sporangia are borne at the tip of the fertile frond on reduced pinnae given over totally to spore production. These sporing tips are brown for the later part of the season

Osmunda regalis 'Purpurascens'

and stand conspicuously against the green of the other foliage. With the onset of the first frosts the foliage turns a buttery golden colour; although only short-lived, perhaps a week, it is an attractive plus point helping to brighten up autumn. This fern was called the flowering fern because the sporing fronds resembled flowering spikes of astilbe or docks. I prefer the other common name because it truly is a regal plant. Unfortunately *O. regalis* does like wet conditions, being happiest at the sides of lakes, as at Savill Gardens in Windsor Great Park where it is luxuriant and self perpetuating, or in bogs. However, those of us without these conditions can still grow good specimens (see Creating boggy conditions, p.98). If allowed to get too dry the fertile fronds readily shrivel and do not recover, but there is usually no damage to the vegetative fronds. Common.

↕ 1.2–2m/4–6ft

🌿 Deciduous

Z 3

≈≈ Wet

🌐 Europe, including British Isles, Asia

Osmunda regalis 'Cristata'

There are a few cultivars, all worth growing when available. **'Cristata'** AGM, 1–1.2m (3–4ft), is like the type, except the pinnae and pinnule tips are flat crested. This form is usually more compact, with a bushier outline and the sporing spikes are shorter and less conspicuous. Quite rare. This cultivar was discovered among a large batch of plants collected from the wild in 1857 while dormant. A nurseryman bought the entire batch from the fern dealer, but it was only in the following spring that one plant produced crested fronds and was noticed by a great fern man, Dr G.B. Wollaston. He offered £25 (a fortune then) for the plant but his offer was declined. The cultivar comes true from spores and in no time at all it was widely distributed. £25 would buy five plants today. Occasionally sporelings produce a branched stipe and have been called **'Ramocristata'**, or large bunched crests at the top of the fronds and have been called **'Corymbifera'**. **'Purpurascens'**, 1–1.2m (36–48in), is possibly from the Atlantic Isles. The stipe is deep purple and the laminae purple when young, turning green. It is also more delicately divided than normal *O. regalis* with smaller pinnules relatively more widely spaced on the pinna midrib – it could be a different species or subspecies. This form comes almost true from spores, but some plants are less strongly purple. It may be less hardy than the other cultivars, perhaps needing some protection in zones 3 and 4. Common. **var.** *spectabilis*, 1.2–2m (4–6ft), Zone 3, is similar to *O. regalis* except it is a more upright plant, potentially taller. It is transiently red-tinted in spring. This is the North American form. Rare. 'Undulatifolia', syn. 'Crispa', 'Undulata', Europe, not British Isles, 1–1.2m (36–48in), is like the type, except that the lamina, not the rachis, is wavy. Quite rare.

Paesia

New Zealand.
A genus with a single species.

P. scaberula

Ring fern

↕ 30–60cm/12–24in

 Deciduous

Z 7

≈≈ Wet/Dry

⊕ New Zealand

Fronds lance-shaped, tripinnate pinnule segments small and delicate looking. Stipe straight but rachis characteristically zig-zagging. Rhizomes creeping. In its home territory it is a colonizer of waste ground and can be weedy, looking unattractive in dry spells if the fronds become matted. Conversely, in cultivation in colder regions it is not aggressive and forms a very attractive small clump. In my cold Herefordshire garden, the ring fern held its own well in an acid bed I created for rhododendrons. Rare.

Pellaea

Tropical and warm temperate regions, with a few cool temperate species.
A large genus of nearly 100 species with several species suitable for growing in an alpine house in Britain. Some species are fully hardy. See *Cheilanthes* for cultural requirements.

P. atropurpurea

Purple cliff brake

↕ 15–45cm/6–18in

⌇ Evergreen

Z 3

≈≈ Dry

⊕ North-east USA

A naturally occurring fertile hybrid between *P. glabella* and *P. ternifolia*. Fronds blue-green, narrowly triangular to oblong, bipinnate. Pinnules narrowly triangular, no scales or hairs. Rachis and stipe black, sparingly hairy. Prefers calcareous conditions, preferably limestone rock. Despite the fact that it comes from very cold areas of North America I find this difficult in cultivation. I think it would be best suited to a sheltered cleft between two rocks or with the crown protected by an overhanging rock. Rare.

Phegopteris

Throughout northern temperate regions.
A small group of deciduous ferns often lumped into the large, mainly tropical, genus *Thelypteris*.

P. connectilis, syn. *Thelypteris phegopteris*

Beech fern

↕ 15–38cm/6–15in

⌇ Deciduous

Z 2

≈≈ Wet/Dry

⊕ Europe, including British Isles, North America, Asia

Fronds produced singly on creeping rhizomes, pale green, ovate, pinnate-pinnatifid with a long stipe. Lamina typically longer than broad. The basal pair of pinnae are not connected to adjacent pinnae and are slightly shorter than those immediately above, characteristically pointing forward. A strong colony of this fern looks charming on a bank, the fronds facing forward and the very conspicuous basal pinnae. It has been used to very good effect at Branklyn garden in Perth in Scotland where it thrives in a peaty soil. In the wild, beech fern often grows under bracken or among wet, shady, acidic rocks. Quite rare.

↕	38cm/15in
🌿	Deciduous
Z	5
≋	Wet/Dry
🌐	Kashmir to Taiwan, Japan

P. decursive-pinnata, syn. *Thelypteris decursive-pinnata*
Japanese beech fern
Fronds pale green, pinnatifid, lance-shaped. Pinnae shorten towards frond base, stipe quite long. Pinnae deeply serrate. Rhizomes grow slowly horizontally, gradually forming a clump. Common.

Pneumatopteris

New Zealand.
A genus closely related to *Thelypteris*. There is one species in cultivation.

↕	60–90cm/24–36in
🌿	Deciduous
Z	9
≋	Wet/Dry
🌐	New Zealand

P. pennigera
Fronds lance-shaped, pinnate with linear pinnae lobed almost halfway to midrib. An attractive yellow-green. Hardy in my unheated polytunnels. Included here because it sometimes appears spontaneously on trunks of newly imported tree ferns. Surely hardy in sheltered gardens in south-west England and Eire. Rare.

Polypodium

Cosmopolitan, from tropics to cool temperate regions.
A large genus, many species being hardy in cool temperate areas. Although they are rather similar to one another at a glance, certain species have given us a wonderful range of cultivars far exceeding the beauty of typical wild plants. Once a large genus, *Polypodium* is now relatively small with many previous members now put into newer genera, such as *Microsorium* and *Pyrrosia*. The species included here all have sori lacking an indusium. All polypodiums have creeping rhizomes.

All hardy polypodiums need good drainage plus free air movement around the fronds. In particularly humid sites the fronds can get too big and heavy and hang down on the soil. Also in too-humid or wet conditions, the fronds may develop black blotching, which can be physiological or a fungal disease.

↕	7–60cm/3–24in
🌿	Wintergreen
Z	6
≋	Dry/Wet
🌐	Europe, including British Isles, Asia, North Africa

P. australe, syn. *P. cambricum*
Southern polypody
Fronds thin-textured, pinnate, broadly ovate, almost triangular, with the second pair of pinnae from the bottom usually the longest. Stipe long, rhizomes creeping and covered in pale brown scales. Fronds produced in late summer-early autumn and persist through winter to disappear late spring-early summer. This is probably the best fern (perhaps even the best herbaceous plant) for fresh green foliage throughout winter; even if severely frosted it bounces back as if nothing had happened. The species is believed to have evolved in the Mediterranean region of Europe where

Polypodium australe
'Cambricum Barrowii'

the summers are hot and dry and the winters wet and warm. Any self-respecting fern prefers warm and wet weather so, not surprisingly, the annual cycle of *P. australe* has adjusted to grow during the warm wet winters. Over the millennia, as the species migrated up the western seaboard of Europe, it retained the characteristic of autumn-winter growth, even in the British climate. It needs a well-drained site and, although not essential, it likes limey soil. That difficult corner in the garden where the builders left all their rubble is often perfect, as this mimics its natural habitat on walls and limestone rocks. In Britain it is uncommon but has a particular affinity with castle walls. Rare.

'Cambricum' AGM is a group of at least seven named, and one or two unnamed, clones. All are top-quality gems. In general, fronds are pinnate-pinnatifid with deeply lacerated pinnae and pointed segment tips. The fronds are always sterile (ie. sori are lacking on the underside), so all forms have to be propagated by division of the rhizome. The various forms differ slightly in detail and need to be well established and well grown before they produce fronds in good character: only then can a realistic attempt be made to name the different clones. Curiously all the forms described here were found before 1894, no new cultivars having been discovered in the wild since. I have split the clones into two sections, which I hope will make identification easier. Rare. **Barrowii section** has thick-textured, almost leathery fronds. Pinnae segments not finely serrated. Fronds almost triangular to narrowly ovate. **Cambricum base section** has thin-textured, almost transparent fronds. Pinnae segments finely serrated. Fronds triangular.

Barrowii section clones
'Cambricum Barrowii', 38–45cm (15–18in), was found at Witherslack in the south of the Lake Distict, in 1874 by T. Barrow. It differs from 'Cambricum Henwood' in having pinnae lamina more twisted, making the frond more three dimensional and spiky. The texture of the frond is more solid and slightly more glossy. Very rare in cultivation, with 'Cambricum Wilharris' often grown as 'Cambricum Barrowii'. **'Cambricum Hadwinii'** was found at Silverdale, north Lancashire by Hadwin in 1875. Unfortunately, I have never knowingly seen this cultivar. It may be extinct. It was a narrow, robust form very similar to 'Cambricum Wilharris'. No collection in the past ever seemed to grow both cultivars so I wonder if they are actually the same plant. Further reason for suspicion is the old records for 'Hadwinii Reversion'. This was a pulcherrimum type (ie. completely fertile), and certain parts of 'Cambricum Hadwinii' apparently reverted to it. I have seen this happen only once – to a pan of 'Cambricum Wilharris'! If my suspicions are correct, by the laws of precedence, 'Cambricum Hadwinii' will be the correct name for 'Cambricum Wilharris'. **'Cambricum Prestonii'**, 20–30cm

Polypodium australe 'Cambricum Prestonii'

Polypodium australe
'Cambricum Wilharris'

(8–12in), was found in a block of limestone pavement at Yelland, north Lancashire in 1871 by Preston. He could not extricate it, so he took the whole block home and gradually grew the fern out of its crevice. Similar to 'Cambricum Barrowii' except the frond is narrowly ovate. The lacerations of adjacent pinnae overlap more strongly, hence this cultivar has been called 'Congestum Preston'. This is in every sense a smaller, more delicate plant than all the other cambricums. **'Cambricum Wilharris'** AGM, 38–45cm (15–18in), was found by 'Wilharris' at Pennard in Somerset in about 1893. I wonder if Wilharris was in fact the Mr Harris who was then Head Gardener at Bristol Zoological Gardens, where a large fern collection was housed – perhaps his Christian name was Wil? I also wonder if this was 'found' in a garden as there is no obvious outcropping of limestone at Pennard. Similar to 'Cambricum Barrowii', with which it is often confused, but differs in being much narrower fronded – the frond is lance-shaped. This is the commonest clone of 'Cambricum' in cultivation, but all are rare. See also under 'Cambricum Hadwinii'.

Cambricum base section

'Cambricum', 38–45cm (15–18in), is of unknown origin; it may have originated in Eire in the nineteenth century. Fronds quite papery, lamina along each pinna slightly twisted, making the frond moderately three dimensional and spiky. One of the most beautiful ferns. Rare. **'Richard Kayse'**, 38–45cm (15–18in), is very similar to the base form but always more spiky and the pinnae are not twisted. Probably the most attractive form of cambricum. Found at Dinas Powys in South Wales by Richard Kayse of Bristol in 1668, and was still in its original locality in 1980, albeit in small quantity. It is on a sheer limestone cliff – out of reach of all but rock climbers – where I hope it will remain for many more centuries. Plants in gardens under this name are parts of the original plant, since it is sterile, and can surely, therefore, lay claim to being among the oldest herbaceous plants in existence. We are not talking about sporelings here, but the original plant. This is the form seen by Linnaeus and named *P. cambricum* by him, but which recent

Polypodium australe 'Richard Kayse'

research has shown to be a cultivar of *P. australe*. As it was named by Linnaeus, some have argued it should be used as the type plant and the species name changed to *P. cambricum*. I reject this because if *P. australe* is changed to *P. cambricum* it makes it very difficult to know which form is being referred to. Rare.

'**Crenatum**', 25cm (10in), has roundly lobed (ie crenate) pinnae margins. Rare. '**Cristatum**', syn. 'Cristatum' (old form), 'Cristatum Perry', 25cm (10in), was found in 1854 by H.S. Perry in County Cork, Eire. The pinnae and the frond tip all carry smallish, curled crests. Frequently the crest at the frond tip is slightly depauperate lacking small pieces of lamina and having an extended spike of midrib at some tips. The terminal crest is usually narrower than the frond lamina. Rare. '**Cristatum Forsteri**', syn. 'Cristatum Clewarth', 'Grandiceps Forster', 25cm (10in), was found in 1876 by 'Jas.' Clewarth in County Clare, Eire. A neat cultivar with large crests at tips of pinnae and frond. The terminal crest is usually broader than the frond lamina. Easily distinguished from 'Cristatum' by the larger crests and the lack of depauperation within the crests. Rare.

Polypodium australe 'Grandiceps Fox'

Polypodium australe 'Hornet'

'**Grandiceps Fox**' AGM, 30cm (12in), was found at Grange-over-Sands in the Lake District by Mrs Fox in 1868. Similar to 'Cristatum Forsteri' except this is a more robust cultivar with larger crests on all terminals. Despite being named 'Grandiceps' the crest is often narrower than the frond lamina; however, this is a large cultivar and the crest is always big. Rare. '**Hornet**', 7–20cm (3–8in), was found by me near Llandudno in North Wales in 1983. It was growing on a limestone cliff among many normal plants of *P. australe* in a private garden. I have no doubt that it was a cultivar naturally occurring in that locality. All pinnae and frond tips are truncate with the midrib protruding like a small horn. Rare. '**Macrostachyon**' was found in the Burren district of western Eire by P.B. O'Kelly early in the twentieth century. The frond is normal except the lamina narrows abruptly and ends with a single long, terminal pinna. Sometimes this cultivar is called 'Caudatum' or 'Longicaudatum' in error. An established plant of 'Macrostachyon' is very attractive with the massed, erect terminal pinnae creating quite an effect. Quite rare. '**Omnilacerum Superbum**', syn. 'Omnilacerum Oxford', 'Omnilacerum Superbum Williams', to 75cm (30in), was found at Tregony in Cornwall sometime before 1897 possibly by J.S. Tyerman, or a Mr Williams. Pinnae lacerated along their length and along the length of the frond although the lacerations are shallower towards the tip of the pinnae and the tip of the frond. A well-grown frond can approach 'Cambricum' in silhouette but it differs by being fully fertile. Probably the tallest cultivar of *P. australe*. Unless well cultivated it can look like a form of *P. australe* with slightly lacerated pinnae at the base of the frond only. Quite rare. There is a form in cultivation called '**Oxford Gold**' which apparently has golden blotches when grown in full sun; I have not seen it. Rare.

'**Pulcherrimum**' means 'most beautiful' – an appropriate name for this group of rather similar cultivars. Fronds regularly bipinnatifid, the ends of the pinna segments not sharply pointed. Segments are close together giving the frond a pleasant yet solid appearance. All moderately well-established plants produce some sori, albeit sometimes sparingly. Sori confirm that the plant is not a Cambricum form. The texture of the frond is relatively thick, also quite unlike Cambricum forms. When well grown, the fronds can become tripinnatifid but may get rather heavy and lie on the ground. There are a few named clones that differ a little from each other.

Rare. **'Pulchritudine'** was raised by E.J. Lowe in late 1884. Along the general lines of 'Pulcherrimum' except the tips of frond, pinnae and segments are slightly crisped giving the frond a slightly concave appearance. The margins of the segments are crenately lobed. Sparingly fertile. This is a beautiful cultivar to which I have given Lowe's old name, based on his short description in *British Ferns* (1890): 'A handsome finely cut variety. Fronds concave 12 x 4½in ...' This is not a lot to go on but no other description fits this beautiful fern which I feel sure must have been in cultivation for many years. Rare.

Polypodium australe
'Semilacerum Robustum'

‡ 45–60cm/18–24in

🍃 Evergreen

Z 6

〰 Dry

🌐 Western North America

'Semilacerum', syn. 'Hibernicum' There have been many finds of this form, indeed many good wild populations of *P. australe* support occasional plants of this type. Semilacerum means half lacerated, and fronds in character are irregularly bipinnatifid along the lower half of the frond and normal along the top half. Wild finds can be poor when found but in cultivation they often settle down into interesting plants. First named 'Semilacerum' by Link in 1841. Rare. Some of the best named forms are: **'Semilacerum Falcatum O'Kelly'**, 45–60cm (18–24in), found in County Clare, Eire by O'Kelly around the beginning of the twentieth century. The fronds are lance-shaped (uncommon in *P. australe*), and the pinnae are sickle-shaped (falcate) and curved towards the tip of the frond. The bipinnatifid pinnae can extend more than halfway up the frond in well-grown specimens. This is a beautiful fern; the arching fronds somehow give a feeling of movement. Rare. **'Semilacerum Robustum'**, 45–60cm (18–24in), found on Whitbarrow in the south of the Lake District by Barnes in 1863. A large robust form of 'Semilacerum'. Lacerations deep and quite regular. Tall, erect grower. Rare.

P. glycyrrhiza, syn. *P. vulgare* 'Acuminatum'
Licorice fern
Frond bipinnatifid, darkish green, papery texture, erect. Sori quite small, dark orange-brown when ripe. Pinnae tips acuminate. The rhizome tastes of licorice if chewed. Believed to have been used by west coast Indians as a sweetener for food. Rare. There is a species in Japan, *P. fauriei*, which is superficially similar.

Polypodium glycyrrhiza 'Malahatense', fertile form (left), *P. australe* 'Cabricum' (right)

Polypodium interjectum
'Glomeratum Mullins'

↕ 45cm/18in

🍃 Evergreen

Z 5

≋ Dry

🌐 Europe, including British Isles

↕ 45cm/18in

🍃 Evergreen

Z 5

≋ Dry

🌐 Europe, including British Isles

'Longicaudatum', 25–38cm (10–15in), was introduced into Britain around the time of the First World War. Fronds pinnatifid, each with a long-drawn-out tip. Does not taste as strongly of licorice as the type. Quite rare. 'Malahatense', 25–38cm (10–15in), was found at Malahat in British Columbia, Canada. Fronds bipinnatifid and sterile, along the lines of *P. australe* 'Cambricum'. Not a robust grower with me, new fronds come later in season than normal *P. glycyrrhiza*. There is a rather similar fertile form, which is bipinnatifid but more coarse. It can be identified by the occasional sorus. I am not aware of any name for it. Rare.

P. interjectum

Intermediate polypody

Fronds pinnatifid, narrowly ovate, somewhat leathery. Marginally the longest pair of pinnae is about the sixth pair from the base. Usually a bluish-green. Stipe quite long, produced from creeping rhizomes covered with pale brown scales. Very common in Europe on neutral to lime-rich rocks, walls and banks. In an evolutionary sense this is a modern species which arose as a hybrid between *P. vulgare* and *P. australe*. Rarely on trees. Fronds produced in midsummer. Common. There is one cultivar of garden merit: 'Glomeratum Mullins', 15–22cm (6–9in), was found by Job Mullins, gardener to Lady Oylander, at Beaminster, Dorset in 1873. A curious form with no two fronds the same. Pinnae can be missing or crested, frond tips can be plain or crested. Despite its extraordinary variability it can make an attractive clump in the garden. Propagate by division as it does not come true from spores. Although some spores are viable I do wonder if this is properly a cultivar of *P. x mantoniae*. Rare.

P. x mantoniae

Fronds pinnatifid, narrowly ovate, somewhat leathery, with the longest pair of pinnae usually the fifth or sixth pair from the base. Hybrid betweeen *P. vulgare* and *P. interjectum*. Very similar to *P. interjectum* except the sori never ripen to enclose uniform yellow sporangia; instead the sorus tends to be a mixture of blacks, browns and yellows. Most spores are, therefore, abortive. Included here because the following cultivars are excellent garden plants and the most widely grown polypodiums. Common.

Polypodium x mantoniae
'Cornubiense'

'Bifido-grandiceps', 45–60cm (18–24in), has an obscure history, but it probably arose in cultivation as a hybrid between *P. vulgare* 'Bifido-cristatum' and normal *P. interjectum* early in the twentieth century. A handsome fern with very attractive arching fronds and very robust. Fronds pinnatifid with pinnae ending in flat crests. Crest at tip of frond very wide and flat, more or less in one plane, much wider than the rest of the frond lamina. Abortive spores; propagate by division. Quite common.

'Cornubiense' is of unknown, but quite recent origin. It was unknown in Victorian times unless it is the same as 'Cornubiense Foliosum' raised by Clapham in the nineteenth century. Fronds of two types, normal or bipinnatifid. I have never seen good spores on any of my plants, therefore almost certainly a hybrid. I believe it

↕	20–38cm/8–15in
🍃	Evergreen
Z	7
≈	Dry
🌐	North-west America

↕	30cm/12in
🍃	Evergreen
Z	3
≈	Dry
🌐	Western North America

Polypodium scouleri

↕	38cm/15in
🍃	Evergreen
Z	3
≈	Dry
🌐	Europe, including British Isles, Asia

arose accidentally as a cross between *P. interjectum* and *P. vulgare* 'Elegantissimum', but this is speculation on my part as it has not yet been checked by any scientific technique. Propagation is by division, but because it is a strong grower this excellent cultivar is, fortunately, relatively common. (*P. vulgare* 'Elegantissimum' used to be called 'Cornubiense', but this hybrid has taken over the name. Rather than change the name for what is now a very well-known plant, I propose that this form continues to be called 'Cornubiense' while the original plant reverts to its alternative name of 'Elegantissimum', see below.) Quite common.

P. scouleri
Leather polypody
Fronds pinnate, not broad; pinnae all more or less same length, leathery, shiny on both surfaces, dark green above. Tips of pinnae blunt. In ferns, especially polypods, this leathery texture is common among species from a largely maritime environment. Surprisingly hardy inland in central England, eventually forms a good-sized clump. Rare.

P. virginianum
Fronds pinnatifid, narrowly lance-shaped, very similar to European *P. vulgare*. Apparently not in general cultivation in Europe. Rare.

P. vulgare
Common polypody
Frond pinnatifid, papery, with pinnae shorter than those of *P. interjectum* and more or less the same length for most of the frond. New fronds appear early summer. In nature this is a fern of acid banks and rocks, and also tree branches in high rainfall areas. It is rare for the other species of polypodium to colonize tree branches. In the garden it is not that fussy over soil pH but it does do very well on acid soils, better than *P. interjectum* or *P. australe*. It benefits from planting in a site with good drainage. Common.

'Bifido-cristatum', 30–38cm (12–15in), was found in North Lancashire by Thomas Walmsley in 1867. Fronds pinnate, all pinnae with neat bifid branches forming fan-shaped crests. Terminal crest also a flat fan shape but much wider than the rest of the frond. Strictly speaking a true grandiceps. Comes true from spores. Common. **'Cornubiense Grandiceps'** is like 'Jean Taylor' (below) but lacks any quadripinnatifid fronds. It was first raised by A. Clapham around 1875 and is a hybrid between *P. vulgare* 'Bifidocristatum' and *P. vulgare* 'Elegantissimum'. It comes more or less true from spores but is usually propagated by division. Quite rare. **'Elegantissimum'**, syn. 'Cornubiense', 'Whytei', 30–38cm (12–15in), was found in Cornwall in 1867 by the Rev J.R. Whyte. A remarkable cultivar that produces fronds of three types: perfectly normal fronds, very finely cut tripinnatifid (or even quadripinnatifid) fronds, together with bipinnatifid ones. By happy chance the very finely cut fronds usually predominate. One could be forgiven for thinking that different cultivars have become mixed except careful scutiny will usually reveal two or more characters mixed on the same frond. This is a beautiful fern, but unfortunately rather rare. As far as I am aware it is unique among polypods in occasionally producing bulbils on the upper surface of the frond. So far no-one has succeeded in raising and plants from these bulbils. One frond up to 1cm (½in) long is produced but never any roots. Rare.

Polypodium vulgare
'Jean Taylor'

'Jean Taylor', 7–20cm (3–8in), is a crested form of 'Elegantissimum' from which it was raised by Jack Healey around 1950 and named after his wife. It has the three kinds of fronds but is a bit inclined to be coarse with fewer and fewer quadripinnatifid fronds being produced as the plant ages. Other similar forms have been raised by spores from the same parentage; one recently raised by Robert Sykes has mainly quadripinnatifid fronds and seems more stable. Rare. **'Ramosum Hillman'**, 30–38cm (12–15in), was found in Hampshire by C. Hillman in 1860. Fronds branch near their base, usually into three, and again near the tips. The overall effect is a fan-shaped frond. Was rare in cultivation but recently refound on a wall in Borrowdale in the Lake District. Comes true from spores, but usually propagated by division. Rare. **'Trichomanoides Backhouse'**, 15–30cm (6–12in), was raised at Backhouse's nursery before 1873 as a sporeling of 'Elegantissimum'. Fronds of two kinds: quadripinnatifid or normal. It lacks the intermediate bipinnatifid fronds. Some selections are reputed to produce quadripinnatifid fronds only. This is a gem! Rare.

Polystichum

Worldwide with many species from cool temperate zones.
A large genus including many of the best hardy garden ferns, all of which like good drainage, often with some lime in the soil. Almost all species are evergreen with a fairly leathery texture to the frond. The margins of the pinnae are usually serrated with bristles, appearing spiny, at the tip of each serration, hence *poly – stichum*. The spring croziers of most species are a strong feature, attracting many admiring comments: the curled up tip of the frond is rolled in towards the crown but the weight of the crozier acts to bend the tip of the frond away from the crown, creating a wonderful S-shape in the unfurling fronds, which open in a flush as a spreading shuttlecock. The attraction is further enhanced in a number of species by the presence of abundant scales on the croziers. Most species have short, erect rhizomes.

On the debit side, polystichums can suffer from an unpleasant disease called *Taphrina wettsteiniana*. Fortunately, it is not common but it can get a hold where a lot of polystichums are grown in close proximity, it is quite commonly present on plants of *P. setiferum* in the wild in western Britain. Symptoms are patchy browning and shrivelling of fronds, especially young fronds. It is difficult to control but systemic fungicides sprayed into the crown in early spring, before the croziers start to move, will keep it at bay. Ideally also remove all affected fronds or parts of fronds: this can set the plant back but it should keep the disease in check. As the disease is spread by water, sickly plants can be grown in a greenhouse for a season or two to regain health. Care should be taken not to wet the crown.

P. acrostichoides

Christmas fern
Fronds lance-shaped, pinnate, mid-green. Sporing fronds differ from vegetative fronds by narrowing at the tip where spores are produced. The common name refers to its evergreen nature: it is an attractive plant at Christmas in the northern hemisphere. When the new croziers flush in spring they arch out very distinctively. Easy to grow in a reasonably well-drained site. Common.

 90cm/36in
🍃 Evergreen
Z 3
≈ Dry/Wet
⊕ North-east America

↕ 75–90cm/30–36in

🌿 Evergreen

Z 4

〰 Dry/Wet

🌐 Europe, including British Isles

↕ 60–75cm/24–30in

🌿 Evergreen

Z 6

〰 Dry/Wet

🌐 North-west America

↕ 60–120cm/2–4ft

🌿 Evergreen

Z 7

〰 Dry/Wet

↕ 30–60cm/12–20in

🌿 Evergreen

Z 6

〰 Dry/Wet

🌐 North-west America

↕ 90cm/36in

🌿 Evergreen

Z 6

〰 Dry/Wet

🌐 North-west America

↕ 45cm/18in

🌿 Evergreen

Z 7

〰 Dry/Wet

🌐 Japan

P. aculeatum AGM

Hard shield fern

Fronds lance-shaped, bipinnate, deep green and glossy. Pinnae continue and narrow right to base of frond; stipe therefore very short. Distinguished from *P. setiferum* by the angle at the base of the pinnule where it is attached to the midrib being less than 90 degrees, ie. acute. Young plants and plants in mountainous areas may only develop pinnate-pinnatifid fronds. This form is sometimes called var. *cambricoides*. It can be mistaken for *P. lonchitis*, but in *P. lonchitis* the pinnae are unlobed. Both types are very handsome, forming neat shuttlecocks of spreading fronds. I like to see this fern on a shady bank where the fronds can arch out very elegantly. In the past several cultivars have been described; I believe that all are now extinct or have been reassigned as cultivars of *P. setiferum*. Common.

P. andersonii

Fronds lance-shaped, pinnate-pinnatifid, pale green. Stipe short. Proliferous bud near the tip of most fronds. In my opinion a rather nondescript fern, usually only noticeable for the bud near the frond tips. Quite rare.

P. x dycei

Synthesized hybrid (*P. proliferum* x *P. braunii*) created by Ann Sleep at Leeds University, and named in honour of great twentieth century fern man, Jimmy Dyce. Fronds lance-shaped, bipinnate, mid- to dark green. Stipe very scaly. One or a few bulbils are produced near the tip of the frond. These can form into small plants while still held aloft. Along with *P. munitum* probably the largest polystichum for general garden conditions. Sterile but can be propagated from the bulbils. Rare.

P. imbricans

Very similar to *P. munitum* except pinnae are closer together and often overlap. Fronds stiffly erect, pinnae twisted to nearly right angles with the plane of the rachis. Rare.

P. munitum AGM

Western sword fern

Fronds pinnate, dark green, slightly lax and spreading, with a conspicuous auricle at the base of each pinna on the acroscopic side. One of the larger evergreen ferns and extremely useful in the garden. Forms a loose shuttlecock. **Crisp form** was introduced into Europe by Judith Jones. Pinnae twisted. Fertile. Common.

P. neolobatum

Fronds lance-shaped, dark green, glossy, bipinnate – at least at base. Underside of frond pale green, but also shiny. Pinnules acute-angled at base and tip. Rachis and stipe covered with dark brown scales. Whole frond very tough and rough to the touch. A beautiful garden fern, ideal with its crown planted in the shelter of a rock or stump. Quite rare.

↕	30–45cm/12–18in
⌀	Evergreen
Z	7
≈	Dry/Wet
⊕	Himalaya

↕	60cm/24in
⌀	Evergreen
Z	7
≈	Dry/Wet
⊕	Himalaya

↕	45–60cm/18–24in
⌀	Evergreen
Z	6
≈	Dry/Wet
⊕	Japan

↕	45–90cm/18–36in
⌀	Evergreen
Z	8
≈	Dry/Wet
⊕	Australia

↕	38cm/15in
⌀	Evergreen
Z	6
≈	Dry/Wet
⊕	Japan

↕	75–90cm/30–36in
⌀	Evergreen
Z	5
≈	Dry/Wet
⊕	Europe, including British Isles

P. nepalense

Fronds oblong, pinnate, pinnae not tapering to base of frond. Stipe is about a quarter the length of the lamina. Pinnae not conspicuously toothed and lacking an obvious 'thumb' on the acroscopic side at the base. Pinnae often crisped. Similar to European *P. lonchitis* but distinguished by these details. Rare.

P. piceopaleaceum

Fronds lance-shaped, bipinnate, glossy yellow-green. Pinnules ovate, very few with a basal lobe or thumb, margins bristly. Rare.

P. polyblepharum AGM

Fronds lance-shaped, bipinnate, glossy, yellow-green and covered in golden bristles in spring, gradually turning deep green. Acroscopic pinnules enlarged into a 'thumb'. The golden-bristled croziers in spring are a beautiful feature; the tips are boat-shaped. Fronds spreading when mature. This species is becoming naturalized around at least one garden in Cornwall. Common.

Polystichum polyblepharum

P. proliferum
Mother shield fern

Fronds lance-shaped, bipinnate (approaching tripinnate), dark green. One or a few proliferous buds produced near the tip of the frond. Pinnae narrowly triangular. A beautiful dark green fern, well suited to most gardens. Can produce massive rootstocks with age. Easily multiplied from the bulbils. Quite common.

P. rigens

Fronds lance-shaped, bipinnate, tough, with pinnae tips sharply pointed. New foliage delightfully yellow tinted in spring. When mature, fronds are matt mid-green. They have a distinctive scent, reputedly similar to skunk. Rare.

P. setiferum AGM, syn. *P. angulare*
Soft shield fern

Fronds lance-shaped, bipinnate, light green. Pinnae do not continue to the base of the frond, therefore there is a stipe. Distinguished from *P. aculeatum* by the angle at the base of the pinnule, where it is attached to the midrib, being more than 90 degrees. Fronds arching in the wild type but the cultivars differ widely in this respect. Over 300 cultivars have been described; most are now lost to cultivation and many others not sufficiently distinct to warrant naming. Quite common. **'Acutilobum'**, 60–90cm (24–36in) has sub-erect, lance-shaped, bipinnate, dark green, leathery fronds. Pinnules mostly undivided although some towards the base of the frond have a single lobe or 'thumb'. All pinnules have an acute angle at point of attachment to the pinna midrib. Like 'Divisilobum' below, it is easy to place 'Acutilobum' as a cultivar of *P. aculeatum* by mistake. A very striking cultivar, not as widely grown as it deserves. I have never seen bulbils on true 'Acutilobum'. Rare. **'Capitatum'** occasionally occurs in sowings. Large crest at tip of frond with pinnae uncrested. Rare. **'Congestum'**, 15–25cm (6–10in), has erect, triangular lance-shaped fronds. Rachis short; pinnae

Polystichum setiferum 'Acutilobum'

overlapping. An excellent fern for the front of a border, or rockwork, or even in a trough. The form in cultivation is probably 'Congestum Padley' found by Padley in 1865 in South Devon. I grow another form that I found in Devon about 1980. It has narrowly lance-shaped fronds. Common. **'Congestum Cristatum'**, 15–25cm (6–10in). Spore sowings of 'Congestum' frequently produce a small proportion of crested or ramose plants. The crests are not immediately obvious and do not add greatly to the beauty of basic 'Congestum'. Common. **'Congestum Grandiceps'**, 15–25cm (6–10in) has a broad crest on the frond tip; pinnae crested. Pinnae and pinnules congested. Rare.

Polystichum setiferum 'Cristato-pinnulum'

'Cristato-pinnulum', 90cm (36in), was found by Dr Wills in Dorset in 1878. Fronds lance-shaped, bipinnate, pale green. Pinnules fan-shaped, not crested. Sparingly fertile. Occasionally produces bulbils, although my plants have not produced any for years. Easy to grow and deserves to be more common. Rare. **'Cristatum'** Several different crested cultivars are known. Each has a crest on the tip of the frond and on the pinnae. Only one named clone is believed to be in cultivation at present. Quite rare.

'Dahlem', 75cm (30in), has narrowly triangular to lance-shaped, stiffish fronds, held at around 30 degrees to the vertical, becoming tripinnate. Really a form of 'Divisilobum'. Plants in cultivation are usually sporelings and doubtfully resemble the original clone. This is a fairly new cultivar distributed from Dahlem in Germany. It may be completely new or it may be an old unidentified cultivar given a new name. It is certainly worth growing in its true form as the nearly erect evergreen foliage is a great asset in a fern bed. Common.

Polystichum setiferum
'Divisilobum'

Polystichum setiferum
'Grandiceps'

Polystichum setiferum
'Multilobum'

'Divisilobum' A number of cultivars of *P. setiferum* can be classed as 'Divisilobum'. This is a natural division, based on frond morphology, but over the years it rarely seems to have been understood and has often been confused with 'Multilobum', 'Plumoso-multilobum' and 'Plumoso-divisilobum'. It is not easy to name all individual plants to a specific clone within 'Divisilobum', hence it is convenient to refer to plants as 'Divisilobum' or Divisilobum Group. Common. Named clones include: **'Divisilobum Trilobum'**, syn. 'Caput Trifidum', 'Ramulosum', 45–60cm (18–24in). Re-introduced from North America by Judith Jones in about 1990. Almost certainly an old British cultivar, perhaps taken to Canada by Joseph Wiper around 1900. Fronds triangular or oblong, bipinnate to tripinnate, branching near tip, often into three large heads. Pinnae bifid or flat crested. Abundantly bulbiferous. Rare. **'Divisilobum Wollaston'** was found in a Devon hedgebank in 1852 by G. Wollaston. Fronds spreading, triangular, very neatly tripinnately divided. Usually sparingly proliferous. Plants under this name are common in cultivation but I am unsure how many are true: they are often sporelings which would probably be better named as Divisilobum Group. Common.

'Foliosum Walton', 38–60cm (15–24in), was raised by Walton about 1913. Fronds narrowly triangular, bipinnate, crispy, pale green. Pinnules have serrated margins, they are expanded, overlapping each other, and papery. Fertile. A fine foliose form. Rare. **'Grandiceps'**, 38cm (15in) was first found as 'Grandiceps Talbot' in 1861 in Eire. Fronds erect, narrow, oblong with a large terminal, polydactylous crest. Pinnae gently crested. Pinnules acutely angled at base, reminiscent of *P. aculeatum*. Rare. **'Green Lace'**, 60cm (24in), was raised from spores of 'Plumosum Bevis' in Holland by Cor van de Moesdijk around 1987. Robust with finely cut pinnule sections. It is sterile. Quite rare.

'Herrenhausen', 60–75cm (24–30in), has spreading, triangular to lance-shaped, tripinnate fronds. More leathery and darker green than the species. Like 'Dahlem', a recent introduction from Germany that may actually be a long-lost older cultivar. It seems to come true from spores more commonly than many other cultivars of *P. setiferum* but, nevertheless, not all plants are correctly named. Common. **'Iveryanum'**, syn. 'Divisilobum Cristatum Ivery', 60–75cm (24–30in), was raised in 1870 by Messrs. Ivery. Fronds spreading, triangular to lance-shaped, more leathery and darker green than the species. Neatly tripinnate, crested at tip of frond and pinnae. Often proliferous. Comes more or less true from spores. Many crested forms of 'Divisilobum' are safely placed here. Rare. **'Lineare'**, syn. 'Confluens', 60cm (24in), has been found several times in the wild in the 1870s. Fronds bipinnate, lance-shaped, pale green, slightly leathery. Pinnules linear, and widely spaced. Pinnules confluent at tip of pinnae. A pretty, airy little cultivar. Rare.

'Mrs Goffey', 45cm (18in), was introduced by Reginald Kaye, but I believe the plant was brought to him by a Mrs Goffey. Fronds triangular to ovate, tripinnate, spreading, pale to mid-green. Pinnule segments extremely narrow and delicate in appearance, narrower than in 'Divisilobum'. Here the frond is dense and approaches 'Plumoso-divisilobum'. In the 1960s this was changing hands for £50. It produces occasional bulbils and, while still rare, is in quite a few collections so would be unlikely to reach such a price today. Rare. **'Multilobum'**, 75–90cm

(30–36in), was found in Devon by Robert Gray in 1865. Fronds nearly erect, tripinnate, narrowly triangular or lance-shaped, light green. Usually abundantly proliferous. Pinnulets resemble small versions of the pinnules of the species; in fact, apart from being once more divided, 'Multilobum' is much like the species, whereas in the Divisilobum Group pinnules and pinnulets are narrow and acutely pointed. Decompositum is another group of cultivars so similar to 'Multilobum' that I include it here. There are many minor forms. Quite rare.

'Percristatum', 60–90cm (24–36in), has crested frond tips, pinnae and pinnules. Rare. 'Perserratum', also 60–90cm (24–36in), was first found by Wollaston in South Devon in 1869. It was thought to be extinct until refound by N. Schroder in Sussex in 1972. Frond lance-shaped, bipinnate – or tripinnate at base of pinnae – dark green, glossy, not leathery. Pinnules deeply serrated, with tips of serrations elongated into prominent bristles. A very pretty, somewhat feathery fern. Fertile, comes true from spores. Rare.

Polystichum setiferum
'Plumoso-divisilobum Bland'

'Plumoso-divisilobum', 50–75cm (20–30in), has triangular, quadripinnate, not leathery, light green, very feathery fronds. Divisions of pinnulets narrow, acutely angled at their point of attachment to the midrib, as in 'Divisilobum', hence 'Plumoso-divisilobum'. Fronds not usually as dense as 'Plumoso-multilobum'. The ultimate divisions being narrower give the fern a more airy appearance. There are several selected clones; all are very rare, but all are occasionally proliferous, however, and it is not unknown for bulbils to sport and give new forms. Rare. **'Plumoso-divisilobum Bland'**, syn. 'Divisilobum Bland', 60cm (24in), was found by Bland near Belfast in Northern Ireland around 1910. Fronds quadripinnate at base with pinnae overlapping strongly, tripinnate at top with pinnae not overlapping. This is considered the best wild find in the Divisilobum or Plumoso-divisilobum Groups. Rare. **'Plumoso-multilobum'**, syn. 'Plumoso-densum', 'Densum', 35cm (14in), was raised by Jones and Fox in 1878. Fronds quadripinnate, triangular, not leathery, light green. Divisions of pinnulets are not acutely angled at their point of attachment to the midrib, and resemble very small versions of the pinnules of the species – as in 'Multilobum' – hence 'Plumoso-multilobum'. Bulbiferous when well grown. All parts are highly developed, pinnae overlap each other as do the pinnules, creating a dense, multi-tiered frond. A real beauty which virtually always comes true from spores. It is hard to believe that this fern is a cultivar of *P. setiferum*. The name 'Plumoso-multilobum' is possibly unacceptable as it may not have been coined until after 1959. However, it is a helpful name, advocated by Jimmy Dyce. Common.

Plumosum Group A diverse group of cultivars united by their feathery form and the almost total lack of sporangia, although in exceptional circumstances at least one form ('Plumosum Bevis') can produce spores. **'Plumosum Bevis'**, syn. *P. aculeatum* 'Pulcherrimum Bevis', *P. setiferum* 'Pulcherrimum Bevis', 60–120cm (24–48in), was found in Devon by 'Jno.' Bevis in 1876. Fronds lance-shaped, bipinnate, darkish green, tapering to an almost plaited tip. Pinnules narrow, tapering to an acute angle at point of attachment to the midrib. Usually lacks spores. Bevis was employed to cut the hedgebanks. He noticed this plant was different and took it along to local fern man Dr Wills who immediately confirmed its importance and named it after its finder. For many years this plant was thought to be a cultivar of *P. aculeatum*, but in the 1930s Stansfield started to doubt this, and subsequent

Polystichum setiferum
'Plumosum Bevis'

Polystichum setiferum
'Plumosum Drueryi'

Polystichum setiferum
Ramosum Group

↕ 45–60cm/18–24in

🍃 Evergreen

Z 6

≋ Dry/Wet

🌐 North-west America

↕ 30cm/12in

🍃 Evergreen

Z 7

≋ Dry/Wet

🌐 Korea, China, Japan, Taiwan

---

chromosome counts have confirmed it to be a cultivar of *P. setiferum*. Despite its age, this plant is widely grown – the rootstock splits freely into separate crowns, allowing frequent division, but never freely enough for it to be mass-produced by nurserymen, so it remains a prized collector's fern. It is easy to grow in a well-drained situation. Quite rare. Classification and naming of this fern has long proved difficult. Recently, there has been a move to simplify it to 'Bevis'. **'Plumosum Drueryi'**, syn. 'Pulcherrimum Drueryi', 60–110cm (24–42in), was raised by C.T. Druery around 1900. Sterile. The plant superficially resembles 'Plumosum Bevis' but the pinnules are themselves pinnatifidly divided making it more feathery and even more beautiful. It is very rare and in very few collections. Unlike 'Plumosum Bevis' side crowns are produced only slowly from the rootstock. This plant was raised from the first batch of spores discovered on the normally sterile 'Plumosum Bevis'. **'Proliferum'** is a frequently used name which is now defunct as so many forms of *P. setiferum* are proliferous.

Ramosum Group, 30–45cm (12–18in), is a group of cultivars whose fronds branch several times along their length but do not crest at tips. This sounds unexciting but, in practice, the best are first-class garden plants. The continuous branching of the fronds means they get broader with height, hence the plant is ball-shaped, rather than the usual open shuttlecock. Rare. **Rotundilobum Group**, 30–60cm (18–24in), is a range of cultivars all with rounded pinnules but differing from 'Rotundatum Phillips' by always being slightly irregular with blunt pinnae tips and, usually, heavy cresting and normally bulbiferous. Pinnules serrate. Rare. **'Smith's Cruciate'**, syn. 'Ray Smith', 45–60cm (18–24in), was discovered in a garden by Ray Smith around 1986. Fronds tripinnate, cross-shaped (cruciate), narrow: a cruciate divisilobum. Fertile and bulbiferous. No reference to it has been found in the old literature: thus, it is named in honour of the finder here. Rare. **'Tripinnatum'**, 60–90cm (24–36in), is common in the wild – simply a tripinnate (pinnules cut into pinnulets) form of the normal species. Well-grown plants often develop the tripinnate character. Referred to as 'tripe' by some fern lovers! Rare. **'Wakeleyanum'**, 60cm (24in), was found by a navvy named Russell working on the railway near Axminster in 1860. He donated it to a Miss Wakeley. Fronds oblong lance-shaped, bipinnate, cross-shaped (cruciate), at least in mid-part of frond. The pinnae fork into two equal parts at the point of attachment to the rachis, giving the appearance of a series of crosses along the rachis (see also *Athyrium filix-femina* Cruciatum Group). A rare form that is not usually in good character until a few years old. The original clone probably no longer exists but it comes fairly true from spores as Cruciatum Group. Rare.

P. setigerum, syn. *P. alaskense*
Fronds lance-shaped, bipinnate, mid-green. Pinnules hairy, less prominently stalked than *P. braunii*. Basal acroscopic pinnule enlarged as a 'thumb' (not so in *P. braunii*). Differs from the also similar *P. andersonii* by lacking proliferous buds towards tip of rachis. Another useful garden plant if available. Rare.

P. tsus-simense AGM
Fronds bi- to tripinnate at base of larger pinnae, triangular to broadly lance-shaped, dark dull green, leathery. Pinnae narrow drawn out into a long acutely pointed tip. Pinnule and pinnae sharply pointed. Scales on rachis and stipe black. Forms a small clump. Very pretty and neat. Similar to *P. luctuosum* but the fronds are more finely divided and the pinnae are distant. Common.

↕ 30–90cm/12–36in

🍃 Evergreen

Z 8

≋ Dry/Wet

🌐 New Zealand

P. vestitum
Fronds lance-shaped, bipinnate, dark green and glossy on upper surface. Pinnae well spaced, not overlapping. Pinnules ovate, small, quite crowded on the pinna midrib. Rachis abundantly covered with brown scales. Stipe a quarter the length of frond. A beautiful fern that does well in central England. In the mild, wet climate of north-west Scotland at Inverewe Gardens it flourishes, with fronds up to 90cm (36in) tall. Quite common.

↕ 60–90cm/24–36in

🍃 Evergreen

Z 7

≋ Dry/Wet

🌐 Himalaya, China

P. yunnanense
Fronds narrowly triangular, glossy dark green, bipinnate-pinnatifid. Pinnae quite widely spaced. Pinnules deeply serrated, almost pinnate. Stipe has two types of mid-brown scales and is a third the length of lamina. A very robust grower surviving neglect with style. Even in wet clay this has luxuriated. Rare.

Polystichum yunnanense

Pseudophegopteris
Himalaya.
There are two or three rather similar species in this genus, all probably hardy in zone 7.

↕ 30–45cm/12–18in

🍃 Deciduous

Z 8, possibly 7

≋ Wet/Dry

🌐 Himalaya

P. levingei, syn. *Leptogramme levingei*
Fronds lance-shaped, bipinnate, with pinnules roundly lobed. Pale green, copiously covered with hairs. Rhizomes creeping, potentially invasive but sufficiently attractive to be forgiven. Rare.

Pyrrosia
Mainly tropical with some species from cool temperate regions.
A medium-sized genus, closely related to *Polypodium*. Fronds are normally strap-shaped and leathery. They are usually epiphytic with their creeping rhizomes growing over the surface of tree or tree fern trunks.

↕ 7–15cm (3–6in), larger in wild

🍃 Evergreen

Z 9

≋ Dry/Wet

🌐 Taiwan, China

P. sheareri
Fronds simple, unbranched. Undersides covered with brown hairs. A most attractive species that has survived in my unheated polytunnel for many years now. Much admired for its colour at successive Chelsea Flower Shows. Rare.

Rumohra

Southern hemisphere.
A small genus of one or two species.

R. adiantiformis AGM

Leather leaf

↕ 30–90cm/12–36in

🍃 Evergreen

Z 9, possibly 8

≋ Dry/Wet

🌐 South Africa, Australasia

Fronds triangular, bipinnate-pinnatifid, shiny dark green, very leathery. Rhizomes thick, creeping. Can grow on the ground or on rocks or trees. This is the fern widely sold by florists as long-lasting greenery – it is grown commercially in Florida. It has survived outdoors here for two winters on the trunk of *Dicksonia antarctica*, on which it was imported. Plants I have seen in Australia have always been smaller than South African material. It would be interesting to grow them both side by side. Quite common.

Selaginella

Common in tropics but with several cool temperate species in both hemispheres.
A huge genus of very pretty fern allies. Very unfern-like, often mistaken for a moss. Small, entire leaves are arranged in rows along midrib. Two kinds of spores are produced. Many species would be worth growing but few hardy species seem to be grown in Europe. There are other species from Asia and North America that would probably be hardy in zone 8, but I have never grown them and they are rare in cultivation.

Selaginella kraussiana

S. kraussiana AGM

↕ 2.5–5cm/1–2in

🍃 Evergreen

Z 6

≋ Wet/Dry

🌐 Africa

Ground cover. Pale green leafy stems about 5mm (¼in) wide, branch repeatedly to create an attractive carpet. Sterile leaves of two distinct types. There are many cultivars of *S. kraussiana*, some coloured, which are often available at garden centres. I have not grown them but I expect them to be as hardy as the type. Common. '**Aurea**' has golden-yellow leaves and is more compact than the type. Fully frost hardy. Rare. '**Brownii**' has pale green leaves, forming compact, dome-shaped clumps. Rare. '**Poulteri**' is unremarkable, a rather more straggly form of *S. kraussiana* of garden origin. Rare. '**Variegata**' has creamy white-variegated leaves. Fully frost hardy. Rare.

Thelypteris

Widely distributed but most common in the tropics.
Until a few years ago this genus contained hundreds of species. Recent investigation has, however, removed most to several newly created genera.

↕ 60cm/24in

🍃 Deciduous

Z 9

≋ Wet/Dry

🌐 North America

T. kunthii

Fronds pale green, pinnate-pinnatifid. Reminiscent of *Matteuccia struthiopteris* in form, but unlike that species, its sporing and vegetative fronds are similar. Rare.

↕	45–60cm/18–24in
🍂	Usually deciduous
Z	4
≈	Wet/Dry
🌐	Eastern North America

T. noveboracensis

New York fern

Fronds pinnate-pinnatifid, oblong, yellow-green, with quite a long stipe. Rhizomes creeping and very invasive, not common in European collections. Rare.

↕	60–90cm/24–36in
🍂	Deciduous
Z	4
≈	Wet
🌐	Europe, including British Isles

T. palustris

Marsh fern

Fronds pinnate-pinnatifid, bluish-green, lance-shaped, erect with a long stipe produced at 2–3cm (¾–1¼in) intervals along the creeping rhizomes. Sporing fronds are taller, with pinnae and pinnae segments appearing more slender because the margins are rolled under. The entire undersides of these fronds appear to be covered with the brown sporangia. Can be very invasive but if the space is available it makes excellent groundcover among reeds and suchlike. In drier sites it does quite well and is less invasive, but the fronds are shorter. Altogether not an unattractive garden plant. Quite rare.

Todea

Warm temperate southern hemisphere.
A small genus, related to *Osmunda*. Spores green.

↕	1.2m/4ft
🍂	Deciduous
Z	8
≈	Wet
🌐	Australia, South Africa

T. barbara

Very handsome upright, bipinnate fronds produced on a massive rhizome. A relative newcomer to British gardens and surprisingly hardy so far. Quite rare.

Todea barbara

Woodsia

Mountainous regions worldwide, except for Australasia.
Small alpine ferns ideal in a rock garden or an alpine house. All like good drainage and plenty of light. Foliage flushes early in spring, maturing much earlier than most other ferns. Some species are wintergreen. All bulk up with age, forming an attractive tuft. Woodsias can be recognized when mature by their cup-shaped indusium.

↕	7–15cm/3–6in
🍂	Deciduous
Z	5
≈	Dry/Wet
🌐	Japan, East Asia

W. intermedia

Fronds narrowly lance-shaped, pinnate with some lobing of the basal pinnae. Pinnae hairy. Rare.

↕	15–30cm/6–12in
🍂	Deciduous
Z	3
≈	Dry/Wet
🌐	Eastern North America

W. obtusa

Fronds lance-shaped, bipinnate, light green with a few glands, none on the indusium. Pinnae triangular; pinnules with a rounded tip. A very easily grown species, the one most often seen in collections. Quite common.

↕ 5–15cm (2–6in)

🍃 Deciduous

Z 5

≈ Dry/Wet

🌐 Japan, East Asia

W. polystichoides AGM

Fronds narrowly oblong, pinnate. Each pinna has a small lobe on the acroscopic side at its base, resembling a polystichum, hence its specific name. A very pretty little fern especially in spring when the frond tip hangs down under the weight of the crozier as it unfurls. There is a form of this species in cultivation which is reported to have originated from Kamchatka in Russia. It is very similar but has a slightly shiny upper surface when the fronds are young. Quite rare.

Woodsia polystichoides

Woodwardia Chain ferns

Warm temperate and tropical regions.

Many of the woodwardias are excellent garden plants, often creating a dramatic effect. Chain fern refers to the sori which create a pattern reminiscent of a chain on the upper surface of the pinnule. Woodwardias are closely related to the blechnums and, like that group, prefer an acid or neutral soil, although I have grown *W. unigemmata* satisfactorily in a soil rich in Wenlock limestone. Two of the species listed here, *W. virginica* and *W. areolata*, differ so markedly from the others that they seem completely unrelated, but the key characters of the indusium and the venation show the connection.

↕ 30–60cm/18–24in

🍃 Deciduous

Z 4

≈ Wet or Wet/Dry

🌐 Eastern North America

W. areolata, syn. *Lorinsora areolata*

Fronds pinnatifid, reddish when young, erect on a long stipe. Rhizomes creeping; can be invasive. Fertile fronds similar, except that the pinnae are much thinner, as often seen in species of blechnum. Native to acid bogs in America but it can do well in drier conditions. I try to give it lime-free soil. If supplied with adequate water, it can tolerate full sun. Rare.

↕ 60cm–2m/2–6ft

🍃 Evergreen

Z 8

≈ Wet/Dry

🌐 Western North America

W. fimbriata

Giant chain fern

Fronds pinnate-pinnatifid, lance-shaped, green, even when young. Fronds more or less erect except when very large. They are not so elegantly

Woodwardia fimbriata

elongated, nor do they normally arch over to touch the ground like *W. unigemmata* and *W. radicans*. No bulbils on fronds. A magnificent large, evergreen species, but unfortunately proving difficult to propagate. When more readily available, it should be more widely grown. I have grown it for around ten years outdoors in central England. Initially I was cautious and protected it with straw, but for many years now it has been left unguarded over winter and has thrived. It may prove hardy in zone 7. Quite common.

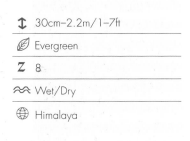

↕ 60cm–1.5m/2–5ft

🍃 Evergreen

Z 9

〰 Wet/Dry

🌐 East Asia to Himalaya

W. orientalis

Fronds pinnate-pinnatifid, ovate with a long stipe. Young fronds green. Upper surface of sporing sections of fronds abundantly covered with bulbils; there are none on the main rachis near the frond tip. Plants sold under this name may be *W. radicans*. I have never succeeded in overwintering this outdoors in central England. Quite rare.

↕ 30cm–2.5m/1–8ft

🍃 Evergreen

Z 9

〰 Wet/Dry

🌐 South-west Europe, including Atlantic Islands

W. radicans AGM

European chain fern

Fronds pinnate-pinnatifid, ovate with a long stipe. Young fronds green. One or more vegetative buds are formed on the main rachis near the tip of the frond. The fronds are arching and tend to touch the ground at this point; the bud then roots and creates a new plant. In this way magnificent thickets of woodwardia can be formed, as at Glanleam in the south-west of Eire. Unfortunately not reliably hardy in central England. Quite rare.

↕ 30cm–2.2m/1–7ft

🍃 Evergreen

Z 8

〰 Wet/Dry

🌐 Himalaya

W. unigemmata

Like *W. radicans* except the new fronds are a beautiful deep red. The colour combined with greater hardiness makes this one of the most sought-after ferns. I grow it with the crown protected by a stone. I have seen this species produce a thicket from the buds near the frond tip in the glasshouses at Edinburgh Botanic Gardens, but I have not seen this happen outdoors as it is relatively new to cultivation. In defiance of the specific name, it does not always have only one bud. In fact there is a possibility that the plant in cultivation is not true *W. unigemmata*: it differs from material first collected in Taiwan in being larger and more deeply bipinnatifid, and in having more than one bulbil. Future research will tell but it is possible that the Himalayan plant should be included in the Philippine species *W. biserrata*. Rare.

↕ 30–60cm/18–24in

🍃 Deciduous

Z 4

〰 Wet/Dry

🌐 Eastern North America

W. virginica

Fronds pinnate-pinnatifid, ovate on a long stipe. Young fronds reddish-brown. Rhizomes creeping; can be invasive. If supplied with adequate water it can withstand full sun. When well grown it is a pretty fern, somewhat reminiscent of *Osmunda cinnamomea*. Rare.

Cyathea dealbata frond underside

Practical projects

Ferns make excellent partners for a wide range of
other plants that like similar growing conditions; they
need not be grown alone. These projects can easily
be adjusted to suit the site by reducing or increasing
the number of plants, or by omitting a few altogether.
They are intended as a starting point and inspiration
for using ferns in imaginative ways.

SHADY SPRING GARDEN

Ferns and shade suit each other very well. In fact, ferns are among the most frequently recommended plants for moderately shaded areas, and many look wonderful in such positions as this is their natural habitat. However, they can merge into a green mass in the shade, especially in a garden filled with colour elsewhere, and this makes it easy to overlook the beauty of their individual fronds. Therefore the best way to use them is in combination with other shade-loving plants that will complement their foliage and form while also ensuring that they get noticed. Hostas, pulmonarias and some hardy geraniums are among the many plants that will do well in a shady site and are perfect partners for ferns as they have attractive foliage and reasonably restrained growth and flowering habits.

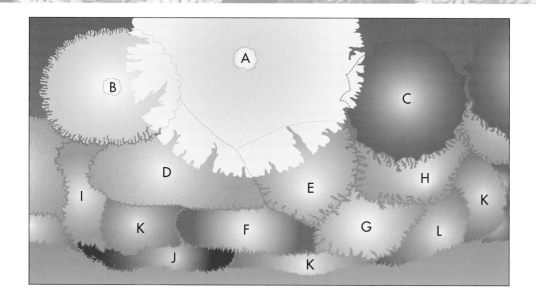

KEY

A *Betula utilis* var. *jacquemontii* AGM – white bark, H to 18m (60ft), S10m (30ft)

B *Acer palmatum* 'Dissectum Atropurpureum' – red-purple leaves, slowly grows to H2m (6ft), S3m (10ft). *A. palmatum* 'Garnet' AGM is similar

C *Choysia ternata* AGM – H/S2.5m (8ft) – don't be tempted by 'Sundance', which will not look good in this situation

D *Athyrium niponicum* 'Pictum' AGM – H38cm (15in), S wide

E *Dryopteris erythrosora* AGM – H60cm (2ft), S38cm (15in)

F *Omphalodes capadocica* AGM – blue flowers early spring, H25cm (10in), S40cm (16in)

G *Hosta* 'Hadspen Blue' – large grey-blue leaves, H25cm (10in), S60cm (2ft)

H *Polystichum setiferum* 'Plumoso-multilobum' – H35cm (14in)

I *Pulmonaria saccharata* – H30cm (12in), or any of its cultivars, such as Argentea Group AGM or 'Leopard' – pink or blue flowers spring

J Snowdrops, such as *Galanthus nivalis* AGM H/S10cm (4in); there are many other species and varieties that are well worth growing

K *Geranium phaeum* 'Samobor' – dark mauve flowers late spring, H80cm (32in), S45cm (18in)

L *Erythronium revolutum* AGM – pink flowers mid-spring, dark brown-mottled leaves, H30cm (12in), S10cm (4in)

This project is designed for a site where there is room to plant the shade-providing backdrop. The scheme is about 5m (16ft) wide by 3.5m (11½ft) deep. Its key season of impact is spring with gentle colour and interest for the rest of the year. In a smaller area that is already shady, the tree and shrubs can be omitted, although this means losing part of the overall effect. Against a fence, for example, ivies can be substituted and, being evergreen, they will provide colour during the winter when many of the other plants have died down. (Train ivies to grow upwards, do not let them run along the ground, where they will swamp ferns.)

The main shade of the scheme is produced by *Betula utilis* var. *jacquemontii* (A), probably the best

Athyrium niponicum 'Pictum'

Dryopteris erythrosora (top)
Polystichum setiferum 'Plumoso-multilobum' (above)

Alternatives

The alternatives listed here are a guide to what could be used to produce similar effects if the plants listed in the key are not available. There are many other plants that would provide slightly different but nonetheless interesting results. For example, *Cotinus coggygria* 'Royal Purple' AGM is a wonderful alternative to the acer, its rounded rich purple leaves creating a softer background for the ferns.

A *Betula pendula* 'Fastigiata' – upright, H20m (70ft), or 'Youngii' AGM – dome-shaped, H8m (25ft)

B *Sambucus nigra* 'Guincho Purple' AGM – elder with leaves of deep purple-green, H6m (20ft) but can be pruned hard to restrict its size

C *Osmanthus x burkwoodii* AGM – leathery evergreen leaves, fragrant white flowers mid-spring, H/S3m (10ft)

D *Athyrium otophorum* – red stipe and veins, H45cm (18in)

E *Adiantum aleuticum* 'Japonicum' – red spring fronds, H45cm (18in)

F *Anchusa azurea* 'Loddon Royalist' AGM – deep blue flowers early summer, H90cm (3ft), S60cm (2ft)

G *Hosta* 'Love Pat' AGM – large blue leaves, H45cm (18in), S 90cm (3ft), or any tall blue-leaved hosta

H *Polystichum aculeatum* AGM, although *P. setiferum* has more filigreed foliage – H/S90cm (3ft)

I *Cyclamen hederifolium* AGM – silver-marked leaves through early spring, pink autumn flowers, H/S13cm (5in)

J *Leucojum vernum* AGM – white spring flowers, H15cm (6in), S10cm (4in)

K *Geranium sylvaticum* – pink-purple late spring-early summer, H75cm (30in), S60cm (2ft)

L *Crocus* – various types available in pink as well as other colours, including yellow, cream, purple

of the white-barked birches. Here it is used as a tree, but it can be coppiced to encourage several trunks to grow, increasing its impact and reducing its eventual height. On either side of the birch are *Acer palmatum* 'Dissectum Atropurpureum' (B) and mexican orange blossom (*Choysia ternata*; C). The acer is a shrubby tree, forming a mound of filigreed purple-red leaves – a delight from spring until autumn – while the choysia has evergreen leaves of a rich green divided into oval leaflets. Its other asset is its white, honey-scented flowers in late spring, which more than make up for the rather acrid smell of the foliage when bruised.

The attractive leaves of the acer and choysia set off the foliage of the ferns. To the left, a ribbon of Japanese painted fern (*Athryium niponicum* 'Pictum'; D) relishes the gentle shade provided by the acer. The

Athyrium otophorum

Disguising ugly corners

Ferns can be used to disguise unsightly areas of the garden, such as the dustbin store or the oil tank for the central heating. These are often in dark dingy corners that many ferns relish. *Dryopteris filix-mas* is particularly good at this job and can be encouraged to grow fresh new fronds halfway through the year, if required, by removing the old ones.

Soil type

Many ferns are not too fussy about soil, although some are more luxuriant in acid conditions. Of the ferns in this scheme, the polystichum has a slight preference for alkaline conditions, while the athyrium and dryopteris should be fine anywhere so long as they have adequate moisture.

athryium, which does best with plenty of moisture, has mauve-red midribs, a colour that seeps into the greyish green of the fronds and is offset perfectly by the leaves of the acer. To the right, the glossy leaves of the choysia give form to the frothy fronds of *Polystichum setiferum* 'Plumoso-multilobum' (H). In the centre is autumn fern (*Dryopteris erythrosora*; E), at its most attractive in spring with the emergence of its pink croziers; as the fronds open they turn bronze before becoming

yellow-green. The snowdrops (*Galanthus nivalis*; J) and lungworts (*Pulmonaria saccarata*; I) frame the emerging fern croziers. Later the American trout lily's (*Erythronium revolutum*; L) pink flowers are beautiful above its rich green brown-marked leaves and against the delicate fern foliage, and then the geranium (*Geranium phaeum* 'Samobor'; K) takes over, the dark splodges at the centre of its leaves adding a touch of class. As the hostas (*Hosta* 'Hadspen Blue'; G) grow, their rolled up cones of blue leaves are beautiful against the foliage of the choysia, opening to form a solid foil for the lighter effects of the ferns.

Among the ferns, the athyrium is deciduous while the polystichum is evergreen and the dryopteris can be more or less evergreen, with yellow fronds usually remaining into late winter and early spring when they are joined by the snowdrops. The athyrium is happiest with plenty of water, so be prepared to provide extra if your soil is free-draining.

Coping with dry shade

Most ferns rely on a reasonably moist site, even if they don't like sitting in permanently damp soil. In nature they are assured of this moisture in their preferred habitats, which are generally under the shade of deciduous trees or among rocks. In the former, the annual leaf fall provides the perfect moisture-retentive soil conditioner, while rocks and stones drip water rather than absorb it so any plants that can get their roots under or around them, especially in sheltered sites, gain a ready supply of water. Imitate nature to give your ferns the best possible growing conditions. Add plenty of compost to planting holes and mulch the planted area at least annually with compost or leaf mould. Consider putting large stones or pieces of wood among the plants to provide cool rootruns.

SUMMER AND AUTUMN BORDER

Ferns are often neglected as possible bedmates for flowering plants in mixed herbaceous borders, yet their contribution can be invaluable. They are excellent for providing texture and subtle foliage colour to tone down bright-flowered neighbours and are particularly useful where the flowering plants have comparatively uninteresting leaves, their fronds disguising this fact and creating lushness where it might otherwise be lacking. Although ferns do best in shady situations, the shade need not be overly obvious. For example, a backdrop of light-coloured shrubs or even simply tall perennials might be all that is required, particularly if the soil is well conditioned so that it retains plenty of moisture, something that most border perennials will appreciate as much as the ferns do.

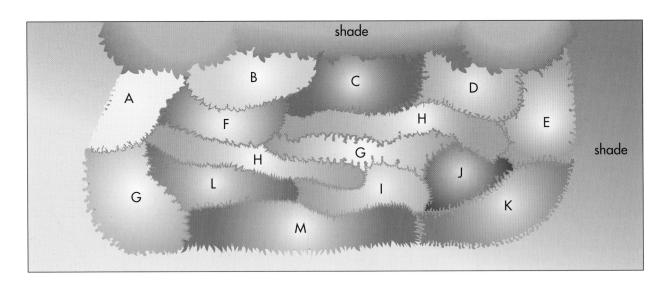

This project is designed for a mixed border of about 7m (23ft) long by 2.5m (8ft) deep. Where there is no existing shade, the shade could be provided by shrubs or small trees whose leaves consist of leaflets or that are variegated. This will provide a light foil for the ferns and other foreground planting (see Shrubs and small trees box, p.94, for some suggestions).

Tall ferns create part of the background in the scheme, the arching fronds of male fern (*Dryopteris filix-mas*; A), lady fern (*Athryium filix-femina*; C) and golden male fern (*Dryopteris affinis*; E) blending well with the feathery foliage of the aruncus (D) and the boldly shaped grey-green leaves

Dryopteris affinis

KEY

A *Dryopteris filix-mas* AGM – H1.2m (4ft)

B *Macleaya cordata* AGM – lobed grey-green leaves, downy undersides, plumes of pale brown flowers in mid- and late summer, H2m (6ft), S1m (3ft)

C *Athyrium filix-femina* AGM – H1.5m (5ft), best in damp soil and dies down with air frosts of autumn so in dry or cold sites consider the alternative

D *Aruncus dioicus* AGM – loose panicles of white flowers early and midsummer, ferny leaves, H2m (6ft), S1.2m (4ft)

E *Dryopteris affinis* AGM – H1.2m (4ft)

F *Actaea simplex (Cimicifuga simplex* var. *simplex)* – feathery leaves, H1–1.2m (3–4ft), S60cm (2ft)

G *Hemerocallis* 'Golden Chimes' AGM – golden yellow flowers early summer, H90cm (3ft)

H *Thalictrum delavayi* AGM – purple petals and yellow-cream stamens midsummer to early autumn, H90cm (3ft) or more, S60cm (2ft)

I *Alstromeria* 'Parigo Charm' – soft pink flowers with yellow and dark markings summer, H1m (3ft), S60cm (2ft)

J *Asplenium scolopendrium* AGM – evergreen, H60cm (2ft)

K *Kirengeshoma palmata* AGM – H1.2m (4ft), S75cm (30in)

L *Polypodium australe* 'Cambricum' – wintergreen, grows new fronds in late summer which persist through to spring, H60cm (2ft)

M *Adiantum aleuticum* – H60cm (2ft)

Alternatives

The success of this scheme relies on particular combinations of foliage shapes and plant forms, and substitute plants inevitably alter the results. If all the alternatives below are used, the effect will be richer and darker with flowers mostly earlier in the year. In this case, except in the case of *Athryrium filix-femina* (see C below), the best alternatives for the ferns are varieties of the species suggested above.

B *Macleaya microcarpa* 'Kelways Coral Plume' AGM
– plumes of coral-pink flowers early and midsummer, H2m (6ft) or more

C *Woodwardia fimbriata* – evergreen, prefers neutral to acid soil, H2m (6ft), plainer than *Athyrium filix-femina*, but more likely to meet with success in colder dryer sites

D *Filipendula purpurea* var. *albiflora* – wide heads of soft white flowers mid- to late summer, H1.2m (4ft), S60cm (2ft) or try *F. purpurea* AGM for pink flowers

F *Actaea simplex* 'Brunette' – dark purplish leaves and stems, white flowers are purple tinted, a rich effect, height similar to species

G Daylilies are available in a variety of colours and many will tolerate some shade, for example, **'Corky'** AGM – yellow, red-backed flowers midsummer, H70cm (28in), S40cm (16in), *H. dumortieri* – orange-yellow flowers early summer, H50cm (20in)

H *Thalictrum aquilegiifolium* – purple-pink fluffy flowers early summer, similar height to *T. delavayi*

I *Alstromeria* 'Margaret' – deep red flowers, H1.1m (3½ft)

K *Heuchera micrantha* var. *diversifolia* 'Palace Purple' AGM – bronze lobed leaves and spikes of pale green flowers in early summer, H/S60cm (2ft); *H.* 'Pewter Moon' is similar with pink-white flowers

of the macleaya (B). Both the aruncus and the macleaya are capable of reaching 2m (6ft) in the right conditions, so they may be taller than the ferns, but their loose forms ensure that they will not dominate. Their flowers are also gentle in form being elegant plumes of white in early summer, in the aruncus, and pale brown and slightly later, in the macleaya. Beside the male fern, the actaea (F), again with white plumes, flowers in early and mid-autumn, easily lengthening the season of interest. Its counterpart near the golden male fern is *Kirengeshoma palmata* (K), a shade-lover with lobed leaves and dark stems carrying pale yellow bells in late summer.

Early in the summer, the front part of the border holds sway with daylilies (*Hemerocallis* 'Golden Chimes'; G), *Thalictrum delavayi* (H) and Peruvian lilies (*Alstromeria* 'Parigo Charm'; I) all working their charm. The thalictrum is particularly beautiful with its puffs of pink and white flowers dotted around the more solid displays of the alstromeria and hemerocallis. It needs good soil otherwise will not fulfill its full potential, fading away to nothing in just a few years, but it repays kindness with delicate but long-lasting blooms.

At the front, hart's tongue fern (*Asplenium scolopendrium*; J), *Polypodium australe* 'Cambricum' (L) and Aleutian maidenhair (*Adiantum aleuticum*; M) have been chosen to disguise the rather boring leaves of the alstromeria and hemerocallis and create an attractive green margin that might spill out onto a path or a gravelled area with equal ease. There are a number of interesting forms of both the hart's tongue fern and the polypody and substituting these would alter the effect. For example, *Asplenium scolopendrium* Crispum Group varieties have fronds with variously ruffled edges that would be particularly attractive against a stone path. The fronds of the Aleutian maidenhair

Asplenium scolopendrium Undulatum Group

are intricately divided and grow in spoked rosettes best seen from above. *Polypodium australe* and its cultivars are valuable in a winter garden as they grow new fronds in late summer and these persist until spring; however, they do look a bit tired by early summer. Although the hart's tongue fern is evergreen, without protection from damaging wind and weather, its fronds are past their best by midwinter. In addition, if the site receives too much sun, they can be scorched. If in doubt, plant it further back in the scheme.

Bulbs and foxgloves

For interest earlier in the year, consider planting foxgloves, weaving them in and out of the groups of perennials, and plant spring bulbs towards the front of the border where they will provide colour in flower and then have their foliage disguised by the ferns and other perennials. For a change from the usual purple foxgloves, choose *Digitalis* Excelsior Hybrids AGM with flowers in pale yellow, white and pink.

Polypodium australe 'Cambricum' (base form)

Shrubs and small trees for the backdrop

Weigela florida 'Variegata' AGM, white margined leaves, H2.5m (9ft), early summer pink flowers

Philadelphus coronarius early summer fragrant white flowers, H3m (10ft); 'Variegatus' AGM leaves with wide white margins

Aralia elata 'Variegata' AGM irregular variegation, H10m (30ft)

Robinia pseudoacacia 'Frisia' AGM H15m (50ft) yellow leaves and fragrant flowers in early summer

Sorbus – many such as *S. aucuparia, S.* 'Joseph Rock' AGM, *S. reducta* AGM

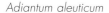

Adiantum aleuticum

WATERSIDE FERNS

Ferns are often associated with waterside situations, although there is only a limited number that thrive in a constantly wet site. Probably the best known of the water-lovers is *Osmunda regalis*, a majestic fern that will survive occasional flooding if this occurs; another is *Onoclea sensibilis*, which spreads rapidly in damp conditions and can even be invasive if it is really happy, although it is an attractive invader that most gardeners would welcome. The fronds of these two ferns are particularly beautiful and have strong distinctive forms so they are able to stand their ground in a mixed planting of other water lovers, which are often coarse plants with bold foliage. Ferns that like water will often tolerate more sun than most, providing they have plenty of moisture.

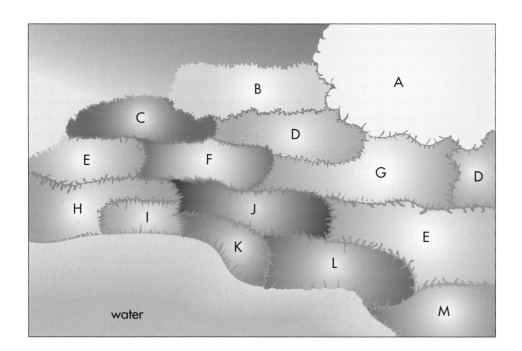

KEY

A *Hydrangea serrata* 'Bluebird' AGM – blue lacecap hydrangea flowers summer into autumn, red autumn leaves, H/S1.2m (4ft)

B *Geranium maculatum* – purple- to bright pink flowers late spring to midsummer, H75m (30in), S45cm (18in)

C *Rogersia pinnata* 'Superba' AGM – palmate leaves, bronzy when young and bright pink flowers mid- to late summer, H1.2m (4ft), S75cm (30in)

D *Dryopteris affinis* 'Cristata' – H1m (3ft)

E *Matteuccia struthiopteris* AGM – H1.5m (5ft), S1m (3ft)

F *Carex oshimensis* 'Evergold' AGM – creamy yellow variegated grass, H/S35cm (14in)

G *Polygonatum x hybridum* AGM – arching stems of green leaves and white pendent flowers late spring, H1.5m (5ft), S30cm (12in)

H *Onoclea sensibilis* – blue-green fronds, pink croziers, H60cm (2ft), S wide

I *Primula florindae* AGM – yellow flowers summer, H1.2m (4ft), S1m (3ft)

J *Astrantia* 'Hadspen Blood' – red pincushion flowers early and midsummer, H1m (3ft), S45cm (18in)

K *Primula beesiana* – candelabras of rich dark pink flowers summer, H/S60cm (2ft)

L *Lysichiton camtschatcensis* AGM – white spathes in early spring, leathery leaves, H/S75cm (30in)

M *Osmunda regalis* AGM – H1.2–2m (4–6ft)

Dryopteris affinis 'Cristata'

This project is intended for a pond or beside a small stream, where the ferns can live on the bank but do not have to spend all their time with their feet in water. The result will be fairly informal: many ferns have a relaxed spreading habit that is most suited to informality or naturalistic effects. The companion plants are included to enhance the filigree foliage of the ferns and ensure that the area is attractive all year round. The area covered

Matteuccia struthiopteris

is approximately 6m (20ft) by 5m (16ft), but can be made smaller by using fewer plants. The scheme assumes a change in level from the water's edge to the back of the planting of about 1m (3ft), but a little rejigging will make it work for a flatter or more steeply sloped site.

On the water's edge sensitive fern (*Onoclea sensibilis*; H) is given plenty of room to spread, its pale pink croziers unfurling in spring in front of the more formal rich green shuttlecocks of ostrich fern (*Matteuccia struthiopteris*; E), which has an echo to the far right of the scheme. Behind the ostrich fern, rogersia (*Rogersia pinnata* 'Superba'; C) has complementary bronzy young leaves that are similar to horse-chestnut foliage. To the right, golden male fern (*Dryopteris affinis*; D) and *Carex oshimensis* 'Evergold' are excellent partners in spring, the evergreen creamy-

Alternatives

If all the alternatives are used, the scheme will have a stronger impact, although perhaps slightly coarser, the flowers mostly in reds and yellows. No alternatives are given for the ferns, as those listed are the most suitable for a waterside scheme. If necessary, *Dryopteris filix-mas* would make a good substitute, though less refined, for *D. affinis*.

A *Hydrangea* – most lacecaps would look good and there are plenty to choose from

B *Geranium* – there are many geraniums in a wide variety of colours, most of which will tolerate this site. Lax varieties such as *G.* 'Ann Folkard' would be particularly effective as the spreading stems ensure flowers appear among immediate neighbours, too

C *Ligularia dentata* 'Desdemona' AGM – brownish leaves and deep orange flowerheads midsummer into autumn, H/S1m (3ft), 'Othello' has purplish leaves

D *Carex elata* 'Aurea' AGM – rich yellow leaves, H60cm (2ft), S38cm (15in)

G *Smilacina racemosa* – upright habit, chunky panicles of white flowers mid- and late spring, requires lime-free soil, H1m (3ft), S60cm (2ft)

I *Primula* 'Inverewe' AGM – red flowers summer, H/S up to 75cm (30in), other **candelabra primulas** are also suitable, providing they grow tall enough; shorter types would be lost unless positioned near the edge of the planting

J *Bergenia cordifolia* 'Purpurea' AGM – evergreen large, thick-textured, rounded reddish green leaves, magenta flowers late winter-early spring, H/S 60cm (2ft)

K *Primula bulleyana* AGM – candelabras of orange-red flowers summer, H/S60cm (2ft)

L *Lysichiton americanus* AGM – yellow flowers and bright glossy leaves, early spring, H/S 1m (3ft)

yellow variegated strappy sedge leaves contrasting well with the ginger-brown unfurling fern croziers; while the arching green stems of Solmon's seal (*Polygonatum* x *hybridum*; G) clothed with rich green leaves and, later, white flowers, make an elegant statement at the left end of the border.

Back down beside the water, giant cowslip and other primulas (*P. florindae*; I; *P. beesiana*; K) form the main focus of the floral display in summer, assisted by the rich pinks of the astrantia (*Astrantia major* 'Hadspen Blood'; J), which has palmate foliage

Osmunda regalis 'Cristata'

Shady notes

For a long-lasting display from the ostrich fern (*Matteuccia struthiopteris*) ensure that it has plenty of shade. Regal fern (*Osmunda regalis*) on the other hand, will survive well in sun, although remaining small, provided it has copious water.

Onoclea sensibilis

not unlike that of the rogersia only smaller. The flowers of all these are quite delicate in appearance, ensuring that they are gentle eye-catchers, and will not draw all the attention from the rest of the planting. The white skunk cabbage (*Lysichiton camtschatcensis*; L) is anything but a gentle eye-catcher, however. Its flowers are the first to appear in spring and are surrounded by pointed white spathes. Although they smell dreadful, they make a good foil for the unfurling fronds of the royal fern (*Osmunda regalis*; M). In fact this bottom corner is the anchor for the planting. Later as the foliage of both matures they produce a strong focal point with their constrasting shapes – the skunk cabbage has oblong veined glossy dark leaves that can reach 1m (3ft) long, while the regal fern has arching feathery fronds almost double that length. At the back, the geranium (*G. maculatum*; B) and hydrangea (*H. serrata* 'Bluebird'; A), are optional, but they do ensure long-term colour and act as a transition into dryer areas away from the water.

Water companions

This design is good next to running water or beside a simple pond, perhaps with a waterlily or two, but there are some aquatic plants that would make suitable companions. *Thalia dealbata* has grey-green leaves and violet summer flowers; it may reach 3m (10ft) in height. *Zantedeschia aethiopica* AGM, arum lily, has glossy arrowhead-shaped leaves and pure white spring and summer spathes; it is about 1m (3ft) tall. *Caltha palustris*, marsh marigold, 40cm (16in) tall, has yellow buttercup flowers in spring and kidney-shaped leaves. It prefers a bankside site. The two flag irises, *Iris versicolor*, blue flag, and *Iris pseudacorus*, yellow flag, are tempting for their attractive iris flowers in summer. However, they can be invasive, particularly the latter, so their vigour will need regular tempering. Blue flag is smaller at 75cm (30in); yellow flag may reach 1.5m (5ft).

Creating boggy conditions

If you have a plastic or concrete pond it is likely that the soil at its edge will be as dry or wet as its immediate surrounds. This doesn't preclude you from planting water-loving specimens, however. It is easy to create the ideal conditions for wet-loving ferns. First, excavate an area to a depth of about 15cm (6in), then lay old compost bags, slightly overlapping, in the bottom of the depression and replace the garden soil, perhaps improved with peat or well-rotted compost. This produces ideal conditions into which to plant moisture-loving ferns. My compost-bag bog enabled me to grow *Osmunda* species and cultivars and other wet-loving ferns very happily. The only problem I encountered was during very dry periods, when they needed additional water as they could not penetrate the plastic layer to root deeper and find water for themselves.

BUCOLIC SPRING BANK

Nature has a way of arranging plants in ones and twos, groups and drifts, so that they look wonderful together. In many parts of the world you can follow a country road in spring and enjoy a huge variety of wild plants mingled together in a verdant display. There is little more pleasing than the sight of primroses, campion, stitchwort, bluebells and fresh fern fronds, which are in abundance at this time of year. Ferns play a major role, particularly the more common species such as *Dryopteris affinis*, *Dryopteris filix-mas*, *Athyrium filix-femina* and *Polystichum setiferum*. They may go unnoticed beside the brighter more frequently recognized country dwellers, but their contribution is important, providing delicacy and structure where the other plants contribute colour.

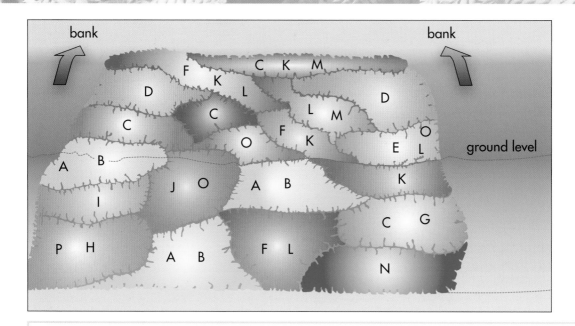

KEY

The plants listed are the native species, or close relatives. Some of these have interesting cultivated varieties that could be tried instead. These are listed where relevant, as are some alternative species.

A *Dryopteris filix-mas* AGM – H1–1.2m (3–4ft), 'Grandiceps Wills' AGM is an eye-catching form and there are others that are equally as interesting

B *Athyrium filix-femina* AGM – H1–1.5m (3–5ft)

C *Asplenium scolopendrium* – H45–60cm (18–24in)

D *Blechnum spicant* AGM – evergreen, H30–45cm (12–18in)

E *Gymnocarpium dryopteris* – H30cm (12in)

F *Viola riviniana* – pale violet-blue flowers late spring and early summer and rounded toothed leaves, H to 20cm (8in), S to 40cm (16in). *Viola cornuta* AGM (Horned violet) – evergreen spring to summer, violet flowers, H7cm (3in), S40cm (16in)

G *Myosotis sylvatica* – biennial, blue, sometimes white, flowers spring to early summer, H30cm (12in), S to 15cm (6in). There are many cultivars that might produce a more refined effect

H *Anemone nemorosa* AGM – pointed lobed leaves, white star-like flowers spring, H to 15cm (6in), S30cm (12in). There are a couple of lovely blue cultivars

I *Convallaria majalis* AGM – lance-shaped leaves and white flowers in arching racemes spring, H22cm (9in), S30cm (12in)

J *Arum italicum* subsp. *italicum* 'Pictum' green-white spathes early summer, orange-red berries, new leaves appear in autumn, better leaves in shade, needs sun to flower well, H30cm (12in), S15cm (6in)

K *Hyacinthoides non-scripta* (English bluebell), blue flowers spring, H25cm (10in), S7cm (3in)

L *Primula vulgaris* – pale yellow flowers mainly from early to late spring, H20cm (8in), S35cm (14in). Double-flowered varieties might provide additional interest but are not so good at fending off competition

M *Silene dioica* – pink flowers spring to autumn, H to 80cm (32in), S30cm (12in). *Lychnis coronaria* (Dusty miller) silver woolly leaves and strongly pink purple flowers late summer, H80cm (32in), S45cm (18in). Requires more light than red campion so may not persist for many years

N *Geranium macrorrhizum* 'Album' – white spring flowers, aromatic, coloured autumn foliage, H45cm (18in), S wide. 'Ingwersen's Variety' AGM is widely grown with clear white-pink flowers spring

O *Digitalis purpurea* – purple spires early summer, H2m (6ft), S60cm (2ft). There are many varieties in a spectrum of colours

P *Ajuga reptans* – groundcover with dark green leaves, spikes of blue flowers late spring to early summer, can be invasive, H15cm (6in), S to 1m (3ft). Various cultivars in different flower or leaf colours

Few of us can create an exact replica of a rural bank, and as they also grow bracken, brambles, hogweed and other coarse species that are not welcome in most gardens, few of us would want to. However, the overall effect is comparatively straightforward to recreate and provides the perfect starting point for a wider range of native plants in the garden. The plan shows plants arranged on a roughly built, stone and earth bank of about 6m (20ft) long by 1.5m (5ft) high with a similar planting area at its base, so that the effect is of the plants spilling off the bank and into the shady surrounds. In the absence of a bank, the whole plan could be interpreted as a flat planting area with the addition of a few large stones to create a naturalistic feel if desired. The soil of the bank can be free-draining but should have plenty of organic material incorporated, otherwise the plants will not thrive. For the same reason, the bank and surrounding area may receive sun for up to half of the day, but needs some shade.

Plants clothe the whole of the bank in small clusters and groups. Along the top bluebells and campion (*Hyacinthoides non-scripa*, K; *Silene dioica*, M) enjoy the good drainage and dappled sunshine in spring.

Planning and planting

The planting plan is deliberately loose as it is best to have informal groupings with plant sizes and shapes interleaved to create the most natural appearance possible. As time passes some groups will take over and will need more rigorous control than others. For example, the bluebells will gradually ease out the woodland forget-me-not and the bugle will choke the windflower. Ensure that the more delicate beauties have a chance of survival by being firm with the good-doers.

They combine well with the bright green new fronds of the hart's tongue fern (remove the battered old ones), which are also perfect partners for the rosettes of the primrose and the dark-leaved diminuitive violet (*Asplenium scolopendrium*, C; *Primula vulgaris*, L; *Viola riviniana*, F). Red campion has a loose spreading form, making a contrast with the more tightly contained shapes of the other plants. Further down the bank, the blechnum and oak fern (*Blechnum spicant*, D; *Gymnocarpium dryopteris*, E) are fernier

Dryopteris filix-mas 'Grandiceps Wills'

in appearance than the hart's tongue fern, again softening the whole effect. The upright sporing fronds at the centre of the evergreen fronds of the blechnum attract the eye – this is a very beautiful fern. Note that the blechnum needs acid soil, while the oak fern prefers it.

At the base of the bank, male fern (*Dryopteris filix-mas*; A) makes an appearance. This common native is frequently under-valued as a garden plant yet it is strongly sculptural, and especially effective with the foxglove (*Digitalis purpurea*; O), and, on top of all this, it thrives in the most unpromising of sites. Here it blends with the elegant lady fern (*Athyrium filix-femina*; B), which has more finely divided fronds. Bluebells have tumbled to the base of the bank, where they do well among the woodland forget-me-not and geranium (*Myosotis sylvatica*; G; *Geranium macrorrhizum* 'Album'; N). Foliage texture is important: the ferns fronds are perfectly set off by the solid shapes of the leaves of the lily-of-the-valley and the arum (*Convallaria majalis*, I; *Arum*

Beware

The plants that have been used in this scheme are natives or close relatives of natives. When purchasing wild plants make sure that they are the genuine article and also that they haven't been taken from threatened wild sources. For instance, in Britain make sure your bluebells are English (*Hyacinthoides non-scripta*), not Spanish (*Hyacinthoides hispanica*), especially if there is a chance that your plants might edge out of your garden into surrounding countryside. As the Spanish bluebell is more robust than the British native and will readily hybridize with it, it represents a real threat to wild populations.

italicum, J). Divided leaves and delicate flowers characterize the windflower (*Anemone nemorosa*; H), which has its brief display in spring, while the bugle (*Ajuga repans*; P) is bolder, its chunky flower spikes looming out from ground-hugging foliage that will spread wherever it is allowed.

Asplenium scolopendrium

EXOTIC FERN FOREST

The basis of this project is tree ferns, which, in their native Australia and New Zealand, usually form part of the understorey in forests of eucalyptus, their palm-tree-like heads of fronds on top of rough brown trunks softening the visual impact of the tall thin trunks of the eucalyptus. In gardens it is not sensible to attempt to reproduce this habitat, but it should be taken into account when incorporating tree ferns. They look best in small, scattered groups of different heights, spaced to allow their fronds room to grow and arch. They also need plants of complementary shapes and sizes with bold foliage to create an exotic feeling of lushness. While flowering plants can play a part, it is more important to achieve the correct balance using strong leaf forms, otherwise there is a danger that the tree ferns will look out of place.

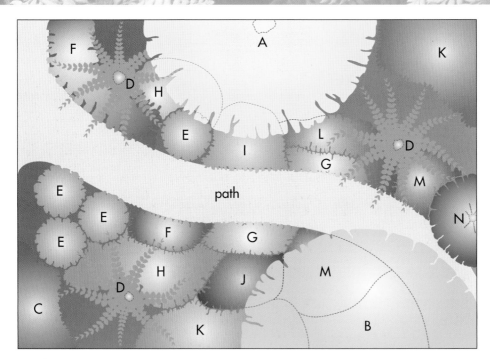

KEY

A *Arbutus unedo* AGM – evergreen foliage, white flowers in autumn, red fruit, peeling cinnamon-brown bark, HS8m (25ft)

B *Eucalyptus pauciflora* subsp. *niphophila* – grey, white and brown peeling bark, blue-green leaves, H/S6m (20ft)

C *Callistemon subulatus* – red flowers mid- and late summer, H1.5m (5ft), S2m (6½ft)

D *Dicksonia antarctica* AGM – H6m (20ft), S4m (12ft)

E *Hebe pinguifolia* 'Pagei' AGM – evergreen blue-green leaves, spikes of white flowers in late spring and early summer, H30cm (12in), S1m (3ft)

F *Epimedium* x *warleyense* – evergreen oval leaves with red tints in spring and autumn, orange-yellow flowers in spring, H50cm (20in), S75cm (30in)

G *Ophiopogon jaburan* 'Vittatus' – wide grass-like leaves striped with white and cream, H60cm (2ft), S30cm (12in)

H *Woodwardia unigemmata* – H1m (3ft), S3m (10ft)

I *Canna*, any hybrid – all have large paddle-shaped leaves and bright late-summer flowers, H to 1.5m (5ft), S to 50cm (20in)

J *Fatsia japonica* AGM – lobed evergreen leaves, heads of white flowers autumn H/S2m (6ft)

K *Phormium cookianum* 'Tricolor' AGM – evergreen strap-shaped pale yellow and red margined leaves, H2m (6ft), S3m (10ft)

L *Carex buchananii* – arching sedge with evergreen rich brown leaves, H75cm (30in), S1m (3ft)

M *Matteuccia struthiopteris* AGM – H1.5m (5ft), S1m (3ft)

N *Cordyline australis* AGM – palm-like tree with evergreen, arching strap leaves, H3m (10ft) or more, S2m (6½ft); 'Purple Tower' has broad, purple leaves

This scheme is intended for an enclosed area, perhaps the whole of a back garden or a separated section of a bigger garden. The feeling of enclosure will help to create the exotic effect: when you enter the area you should feel as if you are in the middle of a jungle. In addition, the enclosure is necessary to provide wind and cold protection for the tree fern fronds and the other less-than-fully-hardy inhabitants. The design fits in an area of about 20m (65ft) by 14m (46ft) with one end (left in the diagram) being sunnier and a little freer draining than the other.

Most of the plants in the scheme are evergreen to a greater or lesser extent, so this is a garden of continuous appeal. In addition there are seasonal flowers and fruit that will provide splashes of colour throughout the year. From autumn and into spring the strawberry tree (*Arbutus unedo*; A) has white flowers set against its evergreen foliage, followed by spherical rough-skinned fruit, the barrenwort (*Epimedium* x *warleyense*; F)

Dicksonia antarctica

produces its discrete orangey flowers in spring with the white flowers of the hebe (*Hebe pinguifolia* 'Pagei'; E) appearing in late spring and early summer. The crimson brushes of Tonghi bottlebrush (*Callistemon subulatus*; C) follow a little later in mid- and late summer. Although the lilyturf (*Ophiopogon jaburan* 'Vittatus'; G) has white flowers in late summer, these are not particularly conspicuous among its white-striped foliage; those of the Indian shot (*Canna* hybrid; I) are brighter and can even be fantastically gaudy, depending on the variety. In the autumn, the humbler flowers of the fatsia (*Fatsia japonica*; J) are attractive although they provide little extra colour.

The tree ferns (*Dicksonia antarctica*; D), the strawberry tree and the snow gum (*Eucalyptus pauciflora* subsp. *niphophila*; B) are the backbone of this garden. Next in importance are the giant reed, the New Zealand cabbage palm (*Cordyline australis*; N) and the New Zealand flax (*Phormium cookianum* 'Tricolor'; K), all of which have a strong upright habit with strap-shaped leaves of

Alternatives

This version relies slightly more on colour with the addition of several brighter flowering plants, such as African lily (G) and red hot poker (I). The effect is richer and warmer.

A *Catalpa bignoniodes* AGM – huge green leaves, white flowers in mid- and late summer then long pods, H/S8m (25ft); 'Aurea' has yellow leaves

B *Pittosporum tenuifolium* 'Silver Queen' AGM – evergreen oval leaves with silver margins, H4m (12ft), S2m (6ft); other cultivars have different colour leaves

C *Grevillea rosmarinifolia* AGM – red flowers late autumn to early summer, evergreen, H3m (10ft), S5m (15ft)

D Other tree ferns could be tried although none is as hardy as *Dicksonia antarctica* – see *Cyathea* and *Dicksonia* in A–Z of Ferns

E *Astelia chathamica* – leaves with silver woolly undersides, pale greeny flowers on long stalks in summer, H60cm (2ft), S1m (3ft)

F *Erigeron karvinskianus* – pink or white daisy flowers in summer, soft-hairy foliage, H30cm (12in), S60cm (2ft) or more

G *Agapanthus campanulatus* – blue bell flowers in rounded umbels atop green stems mid- to late summer, strappy leaves, H1m (3ft), S45cm (18in), best in pots plunged into the soil otherwise often shy to flower

H *Blechnum chilense* AGM – H1.5m (5ft), S wide

I *Kniphofia* 'Jenny Bloom' – pink then cream flowers late summer into autumn, H1m (3ft), S30cm (12in)

J *Melianthus major* – shrub with toothed grey-green leaflets, brown to red flowers late spring to midsummer, H/S3m (10ft)

K *Photinia x fraseri* 'Red Robin' – evergreen shrub with red young leaves, H/S5m (15ft)

L *Stipa tenuissima* – grass with floaty fluffy leaves, H45cm (18in), S30cm (12in)

M *Imperata cylindrica* 'Rubra' – grass with leaves suffused with red, H38cm (15in), S15cm (6in), not ideal for a really shady site

N *Arundo donax* – reed with arching leaves on stout stems, panicles of grassy flowers mid- and late autumn, H5m (15ft), S1.5m (5ft)

different sizes and colours. The leaves and forms of the hebe and bottlebrush create contrasts; the hebe is dome-shaped and neat, while the bottlebrush is loose and sprawling. Complementing the tree ferns are the arching fronds of the chain fern (*Woodwardia unigemmata*; H), which are deep red in spring, and the neat upright shuttlecocks of the ostrich fern (*Matteuccia struthiopteris*; M); these are rich green as they emerge, and will stay this way, providing water and shelter is sufficient. (Consider creating wetter conditions for these two, see box p.98.) Opposite each other either side of the path are the canna and the fatsia. Their large lush leaves underline the exotic nature of the garden. The smaller plants running along beside the path, the lilyturf, barrenwort and sedge (*Carex buchananii*; L), echo other forms in the garden while providing low-level colour and texture.

Woodwardia unigemmata

Winter care

Many of the plants featured in this scheme are not fully hardy, although they should survive in sheltered sites and/or in warmer areas. Success will be difficult where there are long lasting heavy frosts in winter or winters are very wet. Some plants can be brought under cover to overwinter while others will benefit from a mulch in winter or more thorough protection – see p.16.

Environmental concern?

The Convention on International Trade in Endangered Species (CITES) regulates the trade in four dicksonia species from the Americas as well as all cyatheas. Regulation of the harvesting of *Dicksonia antarctica* is no longer deemed necessary. In Australia and New Zealand collection is allowed under approved schemes and most tree ferns come from commercially managed forests (see p.17). The system seems to work well, so British gardeners need not be concerned that their purchase of a *Dicksonia antarctica* will contribute to this species' decline in the wild. However, currently there are fears that alien pests could be imported on tree fern trunks as export checks are not rigorous enough. It is hoped that improved techniques will avoid future problems.

Blechnum chilense

A RIVER OF FERNS

Ferns lend themselves to an informal setting and this is how they are usually used in gardens. However, many have sculptural habits of growth that can be exploited in repeat plantings to make patterns and shapes in the style of a formal garden. Formal gardens, especially knot gardens or parterres, often consist of blocks of plants of one type confined within hedges or paths to produce a symmetrical pattern over a large area. In the right conditions, ferns could be used to create a chequerboard of shades of green. They would be ideal for such use because they have no flowers to alter the effect. Their drawback is their need for shade, while the eventual creeping habit of most means that the planting would require regular maintenance, although all such formal arrangements need hard work to keep them looking their best.

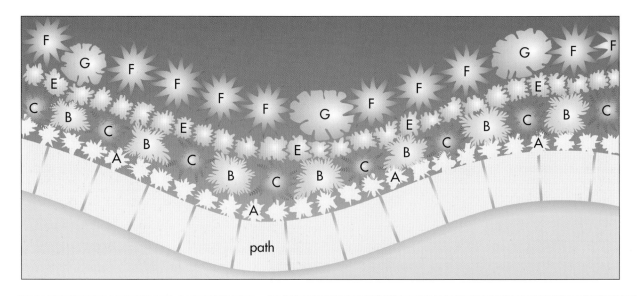

KEY

A *Adiantum venustum* AGM –
  H22–38cm (9–15in)
B *Polystichum polyblepharum* – H60cm
  (2ft); *Dryopteris erythrosora* would
  also be good, pink spring croziers,
  similar height
C *Cyrtomium falcatum* AGM –
  H60cm (2ft), *C. fortunei* is similar
D *Dryopteris sieboldii* – H60cm (2ft)
E *Dryopteris wallichiana* – H90cm (3ft)
F *Polystichum munitum* – H90cm (3ft)
G *Blechnum chilense* – H to 1.5m (5ft)

Adiantum venustum

Polystichum polyblepharum

Dryopteris erythrosora

Alternatives in a wet site

A *Athyrium niponicum* 'Pictum' – H to 38cm (15in)
B *Athyrium otophorum* – fronds last reasonably well into autumn, H to 45cm (18in)
C *Dryopteris cristata* – easy in a damp situation, H60cm (2ft)
D *Onoclea sensibilis* – a keen spreader so be prepared to confine it, H60cm (2ft)
E *Matteuccia struthiopteris* – unbeatable for beautiful rich green shuttlecocks of fronds, H to 1.5m (5ft)
F *Athyrium filix-femina* – dies down with first air frosts, H to 1.5m (5ft)
G *Woodwardia unigemmata* – deep red new fronds, H 2.2m (7ft), but can be smaller; *Woodwardia fimbriata* is slighly smaller, but still attractive, H2m (6ft)

This project is semi-formal. It uses only ferns and relies on their shapes, heights and colours to create a loosley defined pattern. Although it is intended to symbolize a river, the planting could be rearranged to make many other forms, including mathematical shapes such as spirals, squares and triangles. In fact, the possibilities are endless. To ensure success, it is best to cover a reasonable area, otherwise the pattern will not be revealed, and, of course, to ensure the ferns either have plenty of shade or good supplies of water and some shade. Hardlandscaping, such as paths, paving slabs, gravel, bricks and so on, is invaluable to emphasize the lines of the pattern.

Along the near bank of the 'river' runs the delicate beauty Himalayan maidenhair (*Adiantum venustum*; A). This makes excellent groundcover and it can be evergreen in mild winters, while the newly emerging croziers are pink in spring. Its relatively short height ensures that its tracery of fronds can be enjoyed from above, and it is easy to see over to the next ribbon of ferns. This is made up of a mixture of *Polystichum polyblepharum* (B) and Japanese holly fern (*Cyrtomium falcatum*; C). Sharing a similar height and both evergreen, these are very different in appearance. The polystichum has typical ferny

foliage with two key attractions: the croziers are bearded with long golden hairs, and as the fronds unfurl they are a glossy yellow-green. Beside it, the very dark green, sparsely divided fronds of the Japanese holly fern look relatively solid. However, although it looks tough, it may be best protected in cold winter areas. *Dryopteris sieboldii* (D) is an

Hardlandscaping

The plan shows a simple paving-slab path, but other materials would do just as well. Slate chippings are available in purples and blues, which would add to the water-like feeling, while bark would gradually rot down to retain the health of the soil. Single large stones of varying sizes scattered sparingly among the ferns would also be effective in creating the right sort of atmosphere. For the really adventurous, a slope could be planted with a waterfall of ferns, enhanced with carefully placed rocks. To reduce the amount of maintenance required, make the outline shape of the pattern from raised beds of any suitable material, including railway sleepers or bricks. This would prevent the ferns creeping into each other so easily.

optional addition to this area of the river. Reaching about the same height as the other two, it has fronds that are more like Japanese holly fern than another dryopteris. Leathery and pale green, they make a good contrast to the other two species.

Midstream consists of the striking *Dryopteris wallichiana* (E). This is notable for its dark croziers in spring – black because of the heavy covering of brown or black scales on the rachis. This species retains fronds over winter in ideal conditions. Sword fern (*Polystichum munitum*; F) is used to symbolize the water near the far bank. Interspersed with individual plants of the taller *Blechnum chilense* (G), this evergreen species forms shuttlecocks of leathery dark green fronds, which look wonderful beside the statuesque fronds, up to 22cm (9in) wide, of the similarly evergreen blechnum.

Ring the changes

In a reasonably light situation, bulbs such as erythroniums and snowdrops would look wonderful interplanted in ribbons among the ferns. Later in the year, busy lizzies or mimulus might add a splash of colour; both are happy in partial shade and moist-ish sights and come in a range of bright shades. Hostas and other medium-sized foliage plants could be used in place of one or more of the fern varieties, too.

Collections of fern genera could be displayed in patterns. For example, with careful selection, it would be possible to create a square of dryopteris or a circle of aspleniums.

Dryopteris sieboldii

CONTAINER FERNERY

Gloomy courtyards and shady patios are perfect for ferns. These slightly damp, sheltered environments offer suitable growing conditions for a wide range of them, and the shelter they provide ensures that the delicate fronds of many are protected from wind damage. With a little imagination, ferns can be grown alone here, or with any number of other shade-loving plants for company: hostas, ivies, *Hydrangea petiolaris*, *Fatsia japonica* all relish such a site. Pots or raised beds are probably best for ferns in these situations; they are easy in pots, but watering and feeding must be done with care. For a more interesting ferny display, use old tree stumps and chunks of wood to offset the shapes of the ferns. Stumperies – as these are called – date from the Victorian era when they were extremely popular in shady areas, along with plant displays in grottos and on other manufactured rocky outcrops. Somehow, the combination of gently rotting wood and luxuriant fern fronds works extremely well.

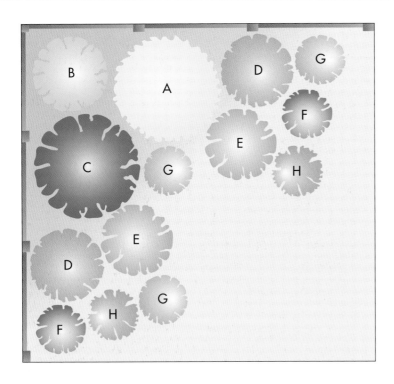

KEY

A *Cyathea australis* – H60cm (2ft) or more

B *Hedera helix* 'Glacier' AGM – grey-green, green and cream variegation, H2m (6ft)

C *Phyllostachys nigra* AGM – black canes and masses of evergreen leaves, H to 5m (15ft), S2m (6ft), clearly less in a pot

D *Athyrium filix-femina* AGM – H1–1.5m (3–5ft)

E *Blechnum nudum* – H60cm (2ft), more when the trunk develops

F *Athyrium otophorum* – H30–45cm (12–18in)

G *Hosta* 'Shade Fanfare' AGM – variegated light green and cream leaves, lavender flowers summer, H45cm (18in), S60cm (2ft)

H *Davallia mariesii* AGM – H22cm (9in)

This scheme is suitable for a corner of a small courtyard or back garden. In this type of site it is a good idea to use a few large specimens to draw your attention and make an effective display. Lots of smaller pots with a wide variety of delicate little plants will be too fragmented and busy, even if it is tempting from a collector's point of view. Once you have a skeleton consisting of larger plants, fill in around it with smaller ferns or other shade-lovers to create a soft understorey or provide punctuation. A benefit of growing ferns in pots is that it is then worthwhile splashing out on more expensive or more tender varieties as they can be appreciated more readily, looked after more carefully and protected more easily in winter than plants in the open garden.

Tree ferns seem to go hand-in-hand with smallish suburban gardens, which tend to be warm and sheltered. Rough tree fern (*Cyathea australis*; A) has been used

Cyathea australis

Courtyard planter with polypodiums

Alternatives

A *Polystichum munitum* AGM – H90cm (3ft), other tree ferns would also be suitable

B There are many **variegated ivies**; it is a matter of selecting one that is attractive but not too rampant

C *Phyllostachys aureosulcata* var. *aureocaulis* – yellow canes to lighten the overall effect, H to 6m (20ft), S wide, but restricted by a pot

D *Polystichum setiferum* and cultivars – smaller than the lady fern at H1–1.2m (3–4ft) at most, but lacy fronds and many cultivars to choose from or collect

E *Woodwardia fimbriata* – H2m (6ft)

F *Athyrium niponicum* 'Pictum' – H38cm (15in)

G As with the ivies, there are literally thousands of **hostas**, each with their own character; choice is simply a matter of taste

H *Paesia scaberula* – H to 60cm (2ft), *Hypolepis millefolium* – H to 38cm (15in), *Onychium japonicum* – H to 45cm (18in)

here, but several other species of tree fern would be worth trying (see A–Z of Ferns, pp.25–85). Their trunks give them a height that is lacking in other ferns and allows other plants to be grown beneath them, creating a third dimension that is often difficult to achieve in a restricted space that is too small for trees. To add to the sense of height variegated ivy (*Hedera helix* 'Glacier'; B) has been trained up an imported tree trunk. This is not an overly vigorous ivy, but even so, protect your fern stock from it by ensuring it only grows upwards. For additional foliage interest and variety, black bamboo (*Phyllostachys nigra*; C) has been included. This elegant bamboo forms a reasonably restrained clump, and is anyway easily restricted by a pot. Lady fern (*Athyrium filix-femina*; D) has much-divided fronds of a wonderfully delicate appearance, making it valuable here, even though it dies down as soon as it receives a touch of frost. It likes a wet site, so is ideal for a pot (see Care, p.114). There are several extremely attractive larger cultivars, which are also well worth trying if available. Fishbone water fern (*Blechnum nudum*; E) is evergreen. This coupled with its neat shuttlecocks of fronds and the fact that it develops a trunk with age, makes it a

Davallia mariesii

good candidate for a pot in full view. Like the lady fern, it needs plenty of water, and it is best in shade; it is not reliably hardy so should be overwintered in a conservatory or greenhouse, or well wrapped up if left outside.

Around these key players, smaller plants provide points of interest and can be added to as necessary. Here, the fresh green fronds of eared lady fern (*Athyrium otophorum*; F) add a splash of colour with their red stipes, while the variegated leaves of the hosta (*Hosta* 'Shade Fanfare'; G) brighten the gloom and create a visual link to the ivy behind. Hardy hare's foot fern (*Davallia mariesii*; H) has been included for its rich green carrot-like foliage. Its short stature makes it ideal for displaying at height, such as in a wall pot or hanging basket, which also means it should not suffer from overwatering.

Care

Ferns can be a little tricky in pots because it is so important to get the watering right. Those that like a wet site or a wet-dry site are reasonably easy because they can be overwatered occasionally (or even stand in water in the case of wet-lovers) without ill effect. Of the first choice ferns, only *Davallia mariesii* needs care in watering, the others simply need good supplies through the growing season. In the alternatives, the polystichums need regular watering, free-draining compost and should never be waterlogged; the hypolepis and onychium are similarly fussy. Like all plants in pots, ferns need feeding. Slow-release granules in the compost and an annual top dressing of the same seem to be sufficient; liquid feed can also be given as a pep.

Covering the soil

Ground cover is useful for maximizing the effect of the display. *Selaginella kraussiana* is a moss-like fern that spreads well in dampish sites and could be encouaged around ferns in pots or raised beds. Baby's tears (*Soleirolia soleirolii*) also excels at such a task. Creeping Jenny (*Lysimachia nummularia*) and its gold-leaved variety ('Aurea') are popular for ground cover, although they can be rather too successful and are somewhat coarse.

Polystichum setiferum 'Dahlem'

Hypolepis millefolium

Appendices

These appendices are intended to help readers interested in learning more about ferns. They contain information on fern hardiness and how cultivars are described, details about a fern's lifecycle, a glossary, notable nurseries and gardens where ferns can be purchased and seen, and a list of further reading.

Appendix I: Hardiness

The zones given in the A–Z (pp.25–85) are based on those defined by the United States Department of Agriculture, which give an estimate of the average annual minimum temperature. They are a rough guide to the climate at a given site; temperatures can vary enormously within a single garden, let alone a region. Severe winters or mild winters will alter the zone rating: my garden in central England is basically zone 8 but in milder winters it is more like zone 9. It is particularly difficult to equate minimum temperatures between dry continental climates and wet oceanic ones; many plants will tolerate lower temperatures in dry conditions, but die when they have to endure cold and wet combined. All ferns included in this book should be hardy in southern Africa and southern Australia.

EUROPEAN PLANT HARDINESS ZONE MAP

The hardiness zone map of Europe is based on one prepared by the Royal Horticultural Society. The zones are defined by the average annual minimum temperatures experienced by the area in question. Plants that are hardy in a particular zone may usually also be grown in all zones warmer than it; for example, a plant that is hardy in zone 6, should survive in zones 7 and warmer. However, the zone system is only a guide. Zone boundaries can only be approximate on such a small scale map. Microclimates within each area may mean you can grow plants from a warmer zone, or conversely, some plants hardy in your zone may not survive in your garden. This is particularly true towards the upper and lower limits of each zone.

USA PLANT HARDINESS ZONE MAP

The USA hardiness zone map shows the hardiness zone system developed by the United States Department of Agriculture. The map works in the same way as the European one (see opposite).

		Fahrenheit	Celsius
Zone 1		below -50°	below -46°
Zone 2		-50° to -40°	-46° to -40°
Zone 3		-40° to -30°	-40° to -34°
Zone 4		-30° to -20°	-34° to -29°
Zone 5		-20° to -10°	-29° to -23°
Zone 6		-10° to 0°	-23° to -18°
Zone 7		0° to 10°	-18° to -12°
Zone 8		10° to 20°	-12° to -7°
Zone 9		20° to 30°	-7° to -1°
Zone 10		30° to 40°	-1° to 4°
Zone 11		above 40°	above 4°

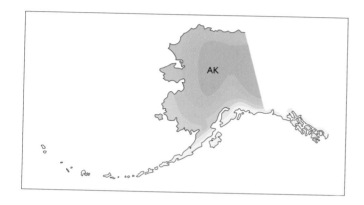

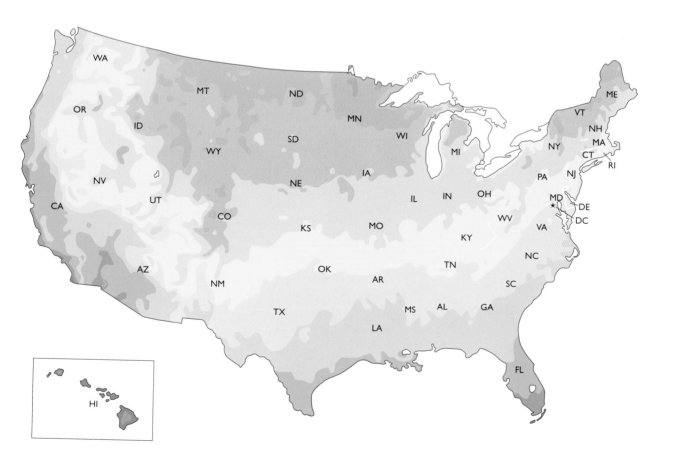

Appendix II: Fern Names and Descriptions

According to the International Code of Nomenclature for Cultivated Plants (first edition 1953), which was established to try to bring some worldwide conformity to nomenclature of cultivated plants, a cultivar named after 1 January 1959 must be named in a living language (ie. not Latin). For example, *Athyrium filix-femina* 'Plumosum Axminster' is an old cultivar. If a new similar but distinct form is raised, it cannot be named, for example, 'Plumosum Cristatum Coke', as 'plumosum' and 'cristatum' are Latin words. To ensure that the affinities between the two cultivars remain clear, however, 'cultivar-group' epithets are allowed. These may be based on an accepted pre-existing Latin-form cultivar name and used in tandem with a new non Latin cultivar epithet. To follow through the example: while *Athyrium filix-femina* 'Plumosum Cristatum Coke' is unacceptable, *Athyrium filix-femina* (Plumosum Group) 'Philip Coke' is acceptable, with or without the part in brackets. Where a completely new break occurs there is not necessarily any need to refer to any previously established group of cultivars.

TERMS USED TO DESCRIBE FERNS

The lists below explain the majority of the terms used to describe fern cultivars.

There are two main divisions: A classifies the fern according to the shape of the frond and B classifies it according to the form of the lamina or pinnae. C is a third, smaller division that contains other variations.

DIVISION A: SHAPE (SKELETON) OF FROND
GROUP 1 *Cristatum* – repeated terminal division or cresting
a) *Capitatum* – at frond apex only.
b) *Cristatum* – at pinnae tips, with or without terminal cresting.
c) *Percristatum* – at pinnae and pinnule tips, with or without apical cresting.
d) *Grandiceps* – crest broader than frond.

GROUP 2 *Ramosum* – major skeletal division
a) *Ramosum* – main leaf stipe (stipe and/or rachis) divides once or repeatedly.
b) *Cruciatum* – secondary leaf rachis (pinnae) divides one or more times at junctions with main stipe.
c) *Brachiatum* – basal pinnae elongate to resemble separate fronds.

GROUP 3 Other
a) *Angustatum* – pinnae greatly reduced in length with narrowed frond.

b) *Deltatum* – pinnae elongated progressively towards frond base to create a deltoid shape.
c) *Parvum* – frond normal in shape but greatly reduced in size.
d) *Congestum* – spacing between pinnae and pinnules reduced, causing overlapping of leafy parts, often combined with brittleness.
e) *Revolvens* or *Reflexum* – pinnae and/or pinnules reflexed, giving frond and/or pinnae a tubular appearance.
f) *Depauperatum* – pinnae and/or pinnules reduced, irregular or missing.

DIVISION B: DEGREE AND FORM OF DISSECTION OF THE LAMINA OR PARTS OF THE LAMINA
GROUP 1 *Dissectum* – margins incised or indented.
a) *Dentatum* – pinnae or pinnules with shallow regular teeth. Further subdivided into Crenatum (teeth rounded) or Serratum (teeth saw-like).
b) *Setigerum* – pinnules indented deeply into narrow segments with pointed teeth or bristles.
c) *Laciniatum* – frond, pinnae or pinnules torn deeply into narrow segments or irregularly pointed lobes.
d) *Incisum* – pinnae or pinnules deeply and irregularly indented.

GROUP 2 *Decompositum* – pinnules subdivided into pinnule-like parts.
a) *Plumosum* – pinnules large and divided one or more times giving feathery appearance; with some exceptions sori absent or scanty.
b) *Tripinnatum* – pinnules enlarged and divided into distinct pinnulets, or merely lobed (throughout whole frond).
c) *Subtripinnatum* – pinnules enlarged and divided into distinct pinnulets, or merely lobed (restricted to parts of frond).

GROUP 3 *Divisum* – pinnules divided; restricted to *Polystichum setiferum*.
a) *Acutilobum* – pinnules narrow, undivided or sharply serrate, very pointed; sharply serrate or undivided but basal lobes distinct, completely or almost separate, narrow, sharply pointed; texture hard; glossy.
b) *Multilobum* – pinnules enlarged, very divided, final segments wide and foliose; texture soft; not glossy, pale to mid-green.
 (i) *Multilobum* – pinnae divided up to three times.
 (ii) *Plumoso-multilobum* – pinnae more enlarged, final segments pinnule-shaped, densely massed and overlapping, building up into a frond thickness of 2cm (¾in) or more.

c) *Divisilobum* – pinnules enlarged, very divided, final segments very narrow, often glossy and dark green.

> **(i)** *Divisilobum* – pinnae divided up to three times, final segments elongated, pointed, texture hard to semi-soft, glossy.

> **(ii)** *Plumoso-divisilobum* – pinnae more enlarged, final segments tend to be slightly wider and softer, semi-glossy; pinnae wide and very overlapping.

d) *Pulcherrimum* – lower pinnules (and rarely the upper ones) greatly extended, slender, sickle-shaped, deeply divided; points run out into slender twisted threads, capable of producing prothalli; texture soft.

e) *Conspicuolobum* – pinnules round, undivided; basal lobes separate and distinct, very round; texture soft.

GROUP 4 *Foliosum* – leafy.

a) *Foliosum* – pinnules wide and leafy, not divided, often overlapping.

b) *Rotundatum* – pinnules broad and rounded.

DIVISION C: OTHER VARIATIONS

GROUP 1 *Rugosum* – blade surfaces leathery and uneven, restricted to *Asplenium scolopendrium*.

a) *Marginatum* – fleshy ridges on under and/or upper frond surfaces, parallel to midrib, usually marginal; often combined with *Muricatum*.

b) *Muricatum* – frond surfaces rough and leathery, covered with short hard excrescences.

GROUP 2 Other pinnule characters.

a) *Crispatum* – pinnules twisted or crisped.

b) *Linearum* – pinnules very narrow and undivided.

c) *Variegatum* – changes in colour.

Appendix III: Glossary

Acroscopic Side of the pinna nearest the frond base.

Antheridia Male sex organ on the prothallus.

Antherozooid Male gamete.

Aposporus Without spores.

Archegonia Female sex organs on the prothallus.

Basioscopic Side of the pinna furthest from the frond tip. See also acroscopic.

Bipinnate Pinnae divided into distinctly separate pinnules.

Bipinnate-pinnatifid Pinnules almost divided into pinnulets.

Crenate Margin roundly toothed.

Crested Forked tips.

Crozier Uncurling frond.

Depauperate Lacking parts of the frond.

Dimorphic Carrying fronds of two types.

Distal Furthest point.

Epiphytic Growing on other plants, using them as a substrate (not parasitic).

Falcate Sickle-shaped, usually meaning that the pinnae are curved towards tip of the frond.

Genus (genera) Term for describing a closely related group of species.

Indusium Flap of tissue covering the sorus.

Lacerate Margin irregularly cut.

Lamina Leaf or frond blade.

Lanceolate Frond lance-shaped – frond broadest between the middle and the base.

Pedate Frond hand-shaped.

Pinna (pinnae) Primary divisions of frond.

Pinnate Frond divided into distinctly separate pinnae.

Pinnate-pinnatifid Pinnae almost divided into pinnules.

Pinnatifid Frond almost divided into pinnae.

Pinnules Divisions of pinnae.

Pinnulets Divisions of pinnules.

Polydactylus Many fingered.

Proliferous Bud bearing.

Prothallus Alternative generation (see Fern Lifecycle p.120).

Rachis Section of the frond midrib that bears the leafy part of the frond.

Rhizome The fern's stem. May be erect as in tree ferns, or creeping as in polypodiums.

Serrate Margin regularly cut into small points.

Sorus The spore-producing structure, includes spores, sporangium and indusium.

Sporangium (sporangia) Structures containing spores.

Spore Dust-like particles which germinate to produce a prothallus.

Sporocarps Spore-bearing structure.

Stipe Midrib of frond below the leafy part (see also rachis).

Stolon A relatively short-lived procumbent stem, usually not swollen and often rooting at the tip to form a new plant. May be above or below ground.

Taxon (taxa) A unit of classification.

Tetraploid Having four sets of chromosomes.

Tripinnate Pinnules divided into distinctly separate pinnulets.

Xerophyte Growing in dry habitats.

Appendix IV: Fern Lifecycle

Ferns have what is called alternation of generations: there are two stages: the sporophyte, which is the plant we see and the prothallus, which produces the gametes. The sporophyte produces spores in the sorus. A mature frond may carry several thousand sori. When mature, the spores are shed and carried on the wind. The sporophyte typically has two sets of chromosomes per cell, but spores have only one set. Those spores that land in a suitable site germinate and grow into a heart-shaped prothallus, which in a short time develops male (antheridia) and female (archegonia) sex organs. The antheridia produce many antherozooids, the male gametes. These are attracted chemically by an archegonium. They swim down the archegonium's neck and the first one in fertilizes the egg cell, the female gamete. The antherozooids and the egg cell have one set of chromosomes each; when they fuse, the complement returns to two sets. (It is clear that the reduction division that occurs when spores are produced is necessary: if there were no reduction division, the number of chromosomes would double in every cell with every additional generation, and the process would not be sustainable.) Once fertilized, the egg cell grows rapidly by normal cell division into a young fern. Depending on the species, it may take from four months to several years before the first true fern frond appears.

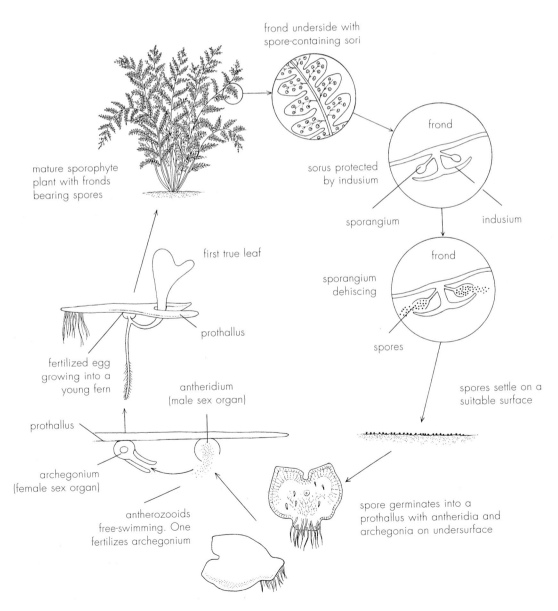

frond underside with spore-containing sori

mature sporophyte plant with fronds bearing spores

sorus protected by indusium

frond

sporangium

indusium

frond

sporangium dehiscing

spores

first true leaf

prothallus

fertilized egg growing into a young fern

antheridium (male sex organ)

prothallus

archegonium (female sex organ)

antherozooids free-swimming. One fertilizes archegonium

spores settle on a suitable surface

spore germinates into a prothallus with antheridia and archegonia on undersurface

Appendix V: Fern Societies

There are many small fern societies scattered around the world. These are best sought out locally, especially as some are short-lived. Larger well-established organizations include:

Australia
The Fern Society of Victoria
This thriving society is centred on Melbourne, where lecture meetings, plant shows and field visits are held. A journal is issued several times a year.
Contact: The Fern Society of Victoria Inc., P.O. Box 45, Heildelberg, Victoria, 3081.

There are several other fern societies in Australia. They are probably best contacted through the Fern Society of Victoria.

Europe
British Pteridological Society
Celebrating its centenary in 1991, this is the oldest fern society in the world and has around 800 members living in about 50 countries and is run entirely by volunteers. Its three journals provide good cover of what is going on in the fern world: the *Fern Gazette*, usually published twice yearly, includes items mainly of specialist interest on international pteridology, the *Pteridologist*, published annually, includes topics of more general appeal, and the *Bulletin*, also published annually, has details of society business and reports. Back numbers of its journals are much sought-after for the valuable information they contain. The society also publishes occasional small books on specialist subjects. Meetings concentrate on lectures, garden visits and expeditions to the more ferny parts of the world. Services to members include a free spore exchange, a book sales scheme (where unusual and rare books are offered at very reasonable prices) and sales of fern merchandise.

In 1998 the Society was greatly honoured when His Royal Highness, The Prince of Wales agreed to be its Patron for a five-year period. The Prince is a great fern-lover with many parts of his garden in Gloucestershire given over to ferns.
Contact: British Pteridological Society, Department of Botany, Natural History Museum, Cromwell Road, London SW7 5BD.

Nederlandse Varenvereniging
This well-organized society holds very good symposia and publishes a journal.
Contact: Mr J. Greep, Van Remagenlaan 17, 6824 LX Arnhem, Holland.

Schweizerische Veriningung der Farnfreunde
I have heard that this is a very friendly, well-run society. It publishes a journal, *Farnblatter*, in German.
Contact: Dr M. Zink, Institut fur Systematische Botanik der Universitat, Zollikerstrasse 107, CH-8008 Zurich, Switzerland.

New Zealand
Nelson Fern Society Inc. of New Zealand
This little society is run by enthusiasts in and around Nelson on South Island. They organize lectures, field meetings and special projects. Most notably they have planted a huge area down to ferns in one of the public parks of Nelson.
Contact: Mrs J. Bonnington, 9 Bay View Road, Atawhai, Nelson, New Zealand.

North America
American Fern Society
Although I have been a member of the American Fern Society for many years I cannot, unfortunately, report first-hand on any of their meetings. I do know, however, they have many field meetings throughout the USA. Their journals are excellent with the *American Fern Journal* covering topics of international Pteridology and the *Fiddlehead Forum* publishing items of more general interest. The American Fern Society was founded in 1893. Contact: David B. Lellinger, 326 West Street NW, Vienna, VA 22180-4151.

Hardy Fern Foundation
This organization takes over the horticultural side of fern interest in the USA. It sponsors fern collections throughout the USA, evaluating hardiness in very wide-ranging conditions, and publishes an excellent quarterly journal. Contact: The Hardy Fern Foundation, P.O. Box 166, Medina, Washington 98039-0166.

There are many other regional fern societies in North America. Details can be obtained through the American Fern Society. Two are listed below.

Los Angeles International Fern Society
A large group with wide-ranging interests. Its journal, *Laifs Fern Journal*, is issued several times a year.
Contact: P.O. Box 90943, Pasadena, CA 91109-0943.

San Diego Fern Society
Although effectively a sub-tropical fern society, its journal is of wide-ranging interest with good information on tree ferns and desert ferns.
Contact: Robin Halley, 1418 Park Row, La Jolla, CA 92037.

Appendix VI: National Collections of Ferns

Since the early 1980s the National Council for the Conservation of Plants and Gardens (NCCPG) has set up National Collections of almost all garden plants grown in British gardens. Similar schemes are run in France and Australia (where as yet no national collections of ferns are recognized) and are being set up in other countries.

Britain

General ferns Savill and Valley Gardens, Windsor Great Park, Windsor, Berkshire SL4 2HT.

British Ferns Alastair Wardlaw, 92 Drymen Road, Bearsden, Glasgow G61 2SY.

Adiantum Tatton Park (National Trust), Knutsford, Cheshire WA16 6QN.

Asplenium Sizergh Castle (National Trust), Kendal LA8 8AE.

Athyrium Nick Schroder, 2 The Dell, Haywards Heath, Sussex RH16 1JG.

Cystopteris Sizergh Castle (National Trust), Kendal LA8 8AE.

Dicksoniaceae Glasgow Botanic Garden, Glasgow G12 0UE.

Dryopteris Harlow Carr Botanic Gardens, Crag Lane, Harrogate, Yorkshire HG3 1QB.

Dryopteris Sizergh Castle (National Trust), Kendal LA8 8AE.

Equisetum Anthony Pigott, Kersey's Farm, Mendlesham, Stowmarket, Suffolk IP14 5RB.

Osmunda Sizergh Castle (National Trust), Kendal LA8 8AE.

Polypodium Harlow Carr Botanic Gardens, Crag Lane, Harrogate, Yorkshire HG3 1QB.

Polypodium Martin Rickard, Pear Tree Cottage, Kyre, Tenbury Wells, Worcestershire WR15 8RN.

Polystichum Joan Loraine, Greencombe Gardens Trust, Greencombe, Porlock, Somerset TA24 8NU.

Polystichum Lakeland Horticultural Society Garden, Holehird, Ullswater Road, Windermere, Cumbria LA23 1NP.

Selaginella Stephan Czeladzinski, Barbican Conservatory, Barbican Centre, Silk Street, London EC2Y 8DS.

France

General ferns (epiphytic) Conservatoire et Jardins Botaniques de Nancy, 100 Rue du Jardin Botanique, 54600 Villers les Nancy.

General ferns Mairie de Paris, Direction des Parcs, Jardins et Espaces Verts, 1 Avenue Gordon Bennett, 75016 Paris.

United States of America

There are no national fern collections as yet but the Hardy Fern Foundation has set up a number of reference gardens across the USA where a wide range of species is grown and documented. The primary study garden is at the Rhododendron Species Botanical Garden in Federal Way, Washington, with satellite plantings at botanical gardens and arboreta throughout the country, from Florida to Alaska. See 'Where to See Ferns'.

Appendix VII: Where to See Ferns

Most, if not all, major cities in the world have a botanical garden where a good selection of ferns is likely to be grown. Those included in this list are known to have a good selection on display. See also 'National Collections of Ferns'.

Australia

Adelaide Botanic Gardens, North Terrace, Adelaide, South Australia 5000.

Australian National Botanic Gardens, G.P.O. Box 1777, Canberra A.C.T. 2601.

Rippon Lea, Elsternwick, Melbourne. Wonderful selection of mainly tree ferns in a Victorian fernery.

Royal Botanic Gardens, Melbourne. Tree ferns luxuriate in a woodland garden.

Sydney Royal Botanic Gardens, Mrs MacQuaries Road, Sydney, New South Wales 2000.

England

In addition to those listed here there are several gardens in Cornwall where tree ferns can be seen outdoors – Trebah, Glendurgan, Carwinion and Penjerrick (all near Mawnan Smith), Trengwainton (near Penzance), and Caerhays Castle and Heligan (on the Roseland Peninsula). In Devon fine examples can be seen at Coleton Fishacre (near Brixham) and Hartland Abbey (near Clovelly).

Many private fern collections are open to visitors by appointment (again see 'National Collections of Ferns'). However, it is the nature of such collections that they get broken up periodically, I have, therefore, not included many in the list.

Abbeydore Court, Abbeydore, Herefordshire HR2 0AD. Hardy ferns in garden.

Brodsworth Hall, Near Doncaster, Yorkshire. Large Victorian outdoor fernery plus quarried area landscaped with tree ferns.

Chelsea Physic Garden, 66 Royal Hospital Road, London SW3 4HS. Ferns in gardens and glasshouses, including research collections.

Greencombe, Porlock, Somerset TA24 8NU. National Collection of *Polystichum* set in one of the most beautiful gardens in England.

Harlow Carr Botanic Gardens (Northern Horticultural Society), Crag Lane, Harrogate, North Yorkshire HG3 1QB.

Knightshayes (National Trust), Knightshayes Court, Tiverton, Devon EX16 7RG. Hardy ferns in gardens.

Lakeland Horticultural Society Gardens, Holehird, Ullswater Road, Windermere, Cumbria LA23 1NP. National Collection of *Polystichum*.

Royal Botanic Gardens Kew, Richmond, Surrey TW9 3AB. Very large collection of ferns, mainly in glasshouses.

Royal Horticultural Society Garden Wisley, Woking, Surrey GU23 6OB.

Savill Garden (part of Windsor Great Park), Wick Lane, Englefield Green, Egham, Surrey TW20 0UU. National Collection of hardy ferns scattered through the garden; beautifully landscaped.

Sizergh Castle (National Trust), Kendal LA8 8AE. National Collections of *Dryopteris*, *Cystopteris*, *Osmunda* and *Asplenium*.

Tatton Park, Knutsford, Cheshire WA16 6QN. Magnificent Victorian tree fern house.

University Botanic Garden Oxford, Rose Lane, Oxford OX1 4AX. Ferns in borders and in glasshouses.

University of Cambridge Botanic Gardens, Bateman Street, Cambridge CB2 1JF. Hardy ferns in garden, also glasshouses.

France

Conservatoire Botanique Nationale de Brest, 52 Allee du Bot. 29200, Brest.

Conservatoire et Jardins Botanique de Nancy, 100 rue du Jardin Botanique, 54600 Villers les Nancy.

Jardin Botanique Parc de la Tête d'Or, Ville de Lyon, Lyon Cedex 06, F-69459.

Mairie de Paris, Direction des Parcs, Jardin et Espaces Verts, 1 Avenue Gordon Bennett, 75016 Paris.

Germany

Arktisch-Alpiner Garten, Schmidt-Rottluff-Strasse 90, Chemnistz, 09114.

Botanischer Garten und Museum, Königen-Luise-Strasse 6-8, 1 Berlin (Dahlem), D-14195. Originator of *Polystichum setiferum* 'Dahlem'.

Munich Botanical Garden, Munich.

Ireland

Many Irish gardens include good stands of *Dicksonia antarctica*, the soft tree fern from Australia. Good examples are Kells House, Kells, Kerry and Dereen Garden, Kenmare, Kerry.

Fota Estate, Cork Harbour, Cork. Good stand of tree ferns including *Dicksonia fibrosa*, and Victorian fernery outdoors.

Glanleam Gardens, Valencia Island, Kerry, Eire. Good range of tree ferns out of doors, also some ground ferns.

National Botanic Garden Dublin, Glasnevin, Dublin 9, Eire. Ferns in glasshouses, including filmy ferns.

Scotland

Glasgow Botanic Gardens, 730 Great Western Road, Glasgow G12 0UE. Ferns mainly in glasshouses, including the National Collection of tree ferns in the Kibble Palace.

Inverewe Garden, Poolewe, Ross-shire IV22 2LG. Mainly ferns in gardens, including tree ferns.

Logan Botanic Gardens, Near Stranraer. Tree ferns and other ferns in gardens.

Royal Botanic Gardens Edinburgh, Inverleith Row, Edinburgh EH3 5LR. Some ferns in garden but most, including a very good collection of tree ferns, in heated glasshouses.

Switzerland

Conservatoire et Jardins Botaniques de Genève, Chemin de l'Impératrice 1, Caisse Postale 60, Chambesy, Genève CH-1292.

Zurich Botanischer Garten, Zollikerstrasse 107, Zurich, CH-8008.

New Zealand

Nelson There is a public park in the centre of Nelson that has a wonderful display of native New Zealand ferns.

Pukekura Park, New Plymouth. Tree ferns and king ferns (*Marattia salicina*) abundant in gardens, with a wonderful range of fern houses including other species – mainly New Zealand natives.

North America

I am indebted to Sue Olsen of Seattle for the very helpful information on the best fern gardens in North America. Sadly I have never visited any of these gardens.

Hardy Fern Foundation (HFF) P.O. Box 166, Medina, Washington 98039-0166, USA.

The Hardy Fern Foundation has sites scattered throughout North America to test the hardiness of different ferns in different areas. At these sites every attempt is made to display and label the plants, as well as keep public records on their performance in the garden. For more information contact the HFF.

The main fern garden is at **Rhododendron Species Botanical Garden**, Federal Way, Washington.

Bainbridge Island Library, Bainbridge Island, WA.

Birmingham Botanical Gardens, 2612 Lane Park Road, Birmingham, AL 35223.

California State University Sacramento, 6000 J Street, Sacramento, CA 95819.

Coastal Maine Botanical Garden, Wiscasset, ME. Dallas Arboretum and Botanical Society, 8617 Garland Road, Dallas, TX 75218. Includes a mist garden.

Denver Botanic Garden, 1005 York Street, Denver, CO 80206.

Georgeson Botanical Garden, 309 O'Neill Building, University of Alaska, Fairbanks, AK 99775.

Harry Leu Botanical Garden, Orlando, FL.

Inniswood Metro Gardens, 940 South Hempstead Road, Westerville, OH 43081.

Lakewold Gardens, 12217 Gravelly Lake Drive, Tacoma, WA 98499.

Les Jardins de Metis, Case Postale 242, Mont Jolie, Quebec, Canada.

New York Botanical Garden, Bronx, NY 104548. Includes Foster Collection.

Rotary Garden, Jaynesville, WI.

Stephen F. Austin State University Arboretum, P.O. Box 13000, Nacogdoches, TX 75962.

Strybing Arboretum, 9th Avenue at Lincoln Way, San Francisco, CA 94122.

University of Northern Colorado, Ross Hall Science Center, Greeley, CO 80631.

Whitehall Historic Home and Garden, Louisville, KY.

The following sites should also be of interest. They are selected from 'A Directory of Fern Gardens, Nurseries and Reserves in the United States, 1994' by Joan Gottlieb, *Hardy Fern Foundation Newsletter*, Vol.4, No.1, Winter 1994.

Atlanta Botanical Garden, P.O. Box 77246, Atlanta, GA 30357.

Bartholomew's Cobble, Weatogue, Ashley Falls, MA 01222.

Bloedel Reserve, 7571 N.E. Dolphin Drive, Bainbridge Island, WA 98110.

Brooklyn Botanic Garden, 1000 Washington Avenue, Brooklyn, NY 11225. A general fern collection and planned Japanese garden with fern glade.

Chicago Botanic Garden, 1000 Lake Cook Road, Glencoe, IL 60022.

Fairchild Tropical Garden, 10901 Old Cutler Road, Miami, FL 33156.

Fern Canyon, Prairie Creek Redwoods St.Pk., 15336 Highway 101, Trinidad, CA 95510. A wonderful ravine with sheer walls covered with adiantums.

Fernwood Botanical Garden, 13988 Range Line Road, Niles, MI 49120.

Garden in the Woods, 180 Hermenway Road, Framingham, MA 01701.

Institute of Ecosystem Studies, Millbrook, NY 12545.

Leach Botanical Garden, 6704 S.E. 122nd Avenue, Portland, OR 97236.

Leonard J. Buck Garden, 11 Layton Road, Far Hills, NJ 07931.

Longwood Gardens, Kennett Square, PA 15221.

Missouri Botanical Garden, P.O. Box 299, St Louis, MO 63166.

Mount Cuba Center, P.O. Box 3570, Greenville, DE 19807.

Norcross Wildlife Sanctuary, 30 Peck Road, Monson, MA 01057.

Planting Fields Arboretum, Planting Fields Road, Oyster Bay, NY 11771.

University of California Botanical Garden, Centennial Drive, Berkeley, CA 94720. Includes an outstanding collection of desert ferns.

University of North Carolina, Charlotte, NC 28223. Specialist *Dryopteris* garden including duplicates from W.H. Wagner Jr. research collection.

Wild Gardens of Acadia, Sieur de Monts Spring, Bar Harbor, ME 04609.

South Africa

Lowveld National Botanic Garden, P.O. Box 1024, Nelspruit 1200.

National Botanic Gardens, Kirstenbosch, near Cape Town. Ferns, including *Cyathea dregei*, flourish in the garden. Above, in Skeleton Gorge, a very good selection of native South African species can be seen in the wild.

Appendix VIII: Where to Buy Ferns

Over the last few years ferns have become more popular with gardeners and, as a consequence, many garden centres and general nurseries offer a reasonable selection. In addition, there are a few specialist retail nurseries. The following are the current principal suppliers. In Britain, the *RHS Plantfinder*, which is published annually, is also a good place to start a search.

Australia

I was fortunate enough to visit Victoria in Australia recently. My impression is that there are few specialist retail nurseries but several trade suppliers to garden centres. Hence, a good collection of ferns is offered at many places. The one specialist I came across was **Fernworld** in Melbourne, which has a wide range of Australian native species, especially tree ferns.

Britain

Fernatics, Ivy Cottage, Ixworth Road, Honington, Suffolk IP31 1QY.

The Fern Nursery, R.N. Timm, Grimsby Road, Binbrook, Lincolnshire LN3 6DH. I have never visited this nursery but the proprietor is a committee member of the British Pteridological Society. Send SAE for list.

Fibrex Nurseries, Honeybourne Road, Pebworth, Stratford-on-Avon, Warwickshire CV37 8XT. Hardy and tender ferns. Also begonias, gloxinias, hederas, hydrangeas, primroses, arum lilies and plants for the cool greenhouse.

Long Acre Plants, South Marsh, Charlton Musgrove, Somerset BA9 8EX.

Mrs Marston, Culag, Green Lane, Nafferton, Driffield, East Yorkshire YO25 0LF. Hardy and greenhouse ferns especially *Adiantum*. Also garden leadwork. Send £1 for catalogue.

Reginald Kaye Ltd., Silverdale, Lancashire LA5 0TY. British ferns and their varieties. The nursery is now run by Reginald Kaye's daughter-in-law and his grandson, Linda and Dominic Kaye. It also grows alpines and hardy perennials.

Rickard's Hardy Ferns Ltd., Carreg y Fedwen, Sling, Tregarth, Near Bangor, Gwnedd LL57 4RP. The nursery is devoted solely to ferns. Most main groups are covered with a special emphasis on tree ferns. Send 5 first-class stamps for a catalogue.

North America

There are many nurseries scattered across North America that sell ferns. The first two given below are the only true specialists, but the others are also excellent sources of ferns.

Fancy Fronds, Post Office Box 1090, Gold Bar, WA 98215. North American and British hardy ferns. Proprietor Judith Jones. Send $2 for a catalogue.

Foliage Gardens, 2003 128th Avenue SE, Bellevue, WA 98005, USA. Wide range of ferns from around the world. Also sells acers. Proprietors Sue and Harry Olsen. Send $2 for a catalogue.

Humber Nurseries Limited, RR No.8, Brampton, Ontario L6T 3Y7, Canada. $2 (Canadian) for a catalogue.

Plant Delights Nursery, 9241 Sauls Road, Raleigh, NC 27603, USA, Send 10 first-class stamps or a box of chocolates for a catalogue.

Rainforest Gardens, 13139 224th Street, Maple Ridge, BC V2X 7E7, Canada.

Russell Graham Purveyor of Plants, 4030 Eagle Crest Road Northwest, Salem, OR 97304, USA. Send $2 for a catalogue.

Siskiyou Rare Plant Nursery, 2825 Cummings Road, Medford, OR 97501, USA. Send $3 for a catalogue.

Appendix IX: Further Reading

Beddome, Col. R.H., *The Ferns of British India*, Madras, 1865–70.

Beddome, Col. R.H., *Handbook to the Ferns of British India*, Thacker, Spink and Co., Calcutta, 1883.

Bolton, James, *Filices Britannicae*, Leeds, 1785.

Boyd, Peter D.A., 'Pteridomania: the Victorian Passion for Ferns', *Antique Collecting*, November 1993, pp.9–12.

Brownsey, Patrick J. and Smith-Dodsworth, John C., *New Zealand Ferns and Allied Plants*, David Bateman, 1989.

Burrows, John E., *South African Ferns and Fern Allies*, Frandsen, 1990.

de Vol, Charles E., et al, *Flora of Taiwan*, Vol. 1, 2nd ed, Epoch, 1980.

Druery, Charles T., *The Book of British Ferns*, Country Life, London (1903).

Druery, Charles T., *British Ferns and their Varieties*, Routledge (1910).

Duncan, Betty D. and Isaac, Golda, *Ferns and Allied Plants of Victoria, Tasmania and South Australia*, Melbourne, 1986.

Dyce, James W., 'Classification of Fern Variations in Britain', *Pteridologist*, 1, 4, pp.154–155, 1987.

Dyce, James W., *The Cultivation and Propagation of British Ferns*, British Pteridological Society, 1993.

Dyce, James W., *Fern Names and their Meanings*, British Pteridological Society, 1988.

Fisher, Muriel E., *Gardening with New Zealand Ferns*, Coolins, Auckland, 1984.

Fraser-Jenkins, Christopher R., *A monograph of Dryopteris in the Indian Subcontinent*, British Museum, London, 1989.

Goudey, Christopher J., *A Handbook of Ferns for Australia and New Zealand*, Lothian, Melbourne, 1988.

Goudey, Christopher J., *Maidenhair Ferns in Cultivation*, Lothian, Melbourne, 1985.

Hall, Nigel and Rickard, Martin H., *A Bibliography of Books and Related Items exclusively about Ferns and Fern Allies appearing before 1900 and written in English*, in press.

Hoshizaki, Barbara Joe and Wilson, K.A., *Fern Growers Manual*, revised and expanded edition, Timber Press, 2001.

Hoshizaki, Barbara Joe and Wilson, K.A., 'The Cultivated Species of the Fern Genus Dryopteris in the United States', *American Fern Journal*, 1999, 1, pp.1–100.

Hutchinson, George and Thomas, Barry A.T., *Welsh Ferns*, Cardiff, 1996.

Jacobsen, W.B.G., *The Ferns and Fern Allies of Southern Africa*, Butterworths, Durban, 1983.

Jermy, A. Clive and Camus, Josephine, *The Illustrated Field Guide to Ferns and Allied Plants of the British Isles*, Natural History Museum, London, 1991.

Jones, David L., *Encyclopaedia of Ferns*, Lothian, Melbourne, and Timber Press, Portland, Oregon, 1987.

Kaye, Reginald, *Hardy Ferns*, Faber and Faber, 1968.

Khullar, S.P., *An Illustrated Fern Flora of West Himalaya*, International Book Distributors, Dehra Dun, 1994.

Khullar, S.P., *An Illustrated Fern Flora of West Himalaya*, Volume II, International Book Distributors, Dehra Dun, 2000.

Large, Mark F. and Braggins, John E., *Tree Ferns*, Timber Press, 2004.

Lellinger, David B., *A Field Manual of the Ferns and Fern Allies of the United States and Canada*, Smithsonian Institution Press, 1985.

Lowe, Edward J., *British Ferns and Where Found*, Swan Sonnenschein, London, 1890.

Lowe, Edward J., *Fern Growing*, Nimmo, London, 1895.

Lowe, Edward J., *Our Native Ferns*, Groombridge, London, 1862–1867.

Mickel, John T., *Ferns for American Gardens*, Macmillan, 1994.

Mickel, John T., *How to Know the Ferns and Fern Allies*, The Pictured Key Nature Series, Iowa, 1979.

Mickel, John T. and Smith, Alan R., *The Pteridophytes of Mexico*, New York Botanic Garden, 2004.

Moran, Robbin C., *A Natural History of Ferns*, Timber Press, 2004.

Newey, Vic, 'Bulbil Production in Lady Ferns', *Pteridologist*, 1, p.115, 1986.

Newman, Edward, *A History of British Ferns*, J. Van Voorst, London, 1854.

Page, Christopher N., *The Ferns of Britain and Ireland*, Cambridge University Press, 1982.

Prelli, Remy and Boudrie, Michel, *Atlas Ecologique des Fougères et Plantes Alliées*, Lechavalier, 1992.

Rasbach, Kurt, Rasbach, Helga and Wilmanns, Ottilie, *Die Farpflanzen Zentraleuropas*, Heidelberg, 1968.

Rickard, M. H., *Ferns*, RHS Wisley Handbook, Cassell 2003.

Rickard, M. H., *The Plantfinder's Guide to Garden Ferns*, David & Charles, 2000.

Rush, Richard, *A Guide to Hardy Ferns*, British Pteridological Society, 1984.

Schneider, George, *A Book of Choice Ferns*, Upcott Gill, London, 1890–1894.

Tagawa, Motozi, *Coloured Illustrations of Japanese Pteridophyta*, Hoikusha, Osaka, 1959.

Index

Page numbers in *italic* type refer to illustrations